THE
LONDON SOLICITORS
GOLFING SOCIETY

A HISTORY 1904–2010

THE
LONDON SOLICITORS
GOLFING SOCIETY

A HISTORY 1904–2010

STEPHEN BARNARD

with contributions from
Jonathan Chalton, F R Furber, Peter Morley-Jacob and others

To my very dear friend Janey, as an esteemed fellow author Stephen Barnard 31 March 2012

PUBLISHED BY
THE LONDON SOLICITORS' GOLFING SOCIETY

First published in Great Britain in 2010
by The London Solicitors' Golfing Society
66 Lincoln's Inn Fields, London WC2A 3LH

A CIP catalogue record for this book is available
from the British Library.

ISBN 978-0-9566113-1-4

Designed in Kingfisher by Geoff Green Book Design, Cambridge
Printed and bound in Great Britain by Henry Ling, Dorchester, Dorset

Contents

Foreword

I T WAS THE APPROACH of the London Solicitors' Golfing Society's centenary that prompted thoughts of compiling this history and cautious steps were taken to put something on record. It was only when things were well under way that I realised, many years before I joined the Society, I had crossed paths with two former distinguished members. Sir Dingwall Bateson, who had been President of the Law Society and had played in the early matches against the Scots, had "advised" me as to my future in the profession. John Haslam, a much loved one time President of Royal Mid-Surrey Golf Club and an important Secretary and Captain of the Society, had offered me a job.

There have been occasions, over the years, when the Society has struggled for support, most notably around the times of the two world wars. Notwithstanding this, there has been, in each generation, a small group of people who have revived it and as a result have provided the continuity which has allowed members to enjoy the company of other golfers, both within and without the legal profession, and to make many and lasting friendships.

Was it just an interest in golf which prompted those solicitors who started our Society? We will never know, but it must surely be true that the Society, once formed, apart from giving members access to golf on many of the great courses around the south of England, also provided the opportunity for social contact between lawyers of differing ages and legal practices.

It used to be said that a great deal of business was transacted on the golf course. However true that may or may not have been, I suspect that not a great deal of useful business is done on a golf course these days but I always found it much easier to deal with another lawyer whom I had met socially or on a sports field than one I had never met before.

We are grateful to quite a few people who have been involved in preparing this history but I must record, as everyone would wish, our particular thanks to Jonathan Chalton and Stephen Barnard. It was Jonathan, who some time before our centenary year was the instigator and initial coordinator and he has also produced many of the photographs. Stephen, when the initial impetus was faltering, was the person who assumed the major role and saw it through to completion.

It is with great pleasure and many happy memories that I write this foreword to congratulate the Society on having passed its first century and to wish it well for the future. Friendship, challenge and fair play abound here.

PETER MORLEY-JACOB

Acknowledgements

WITHOUT THE Secretaries of the London Solicitors' Golfing Society there would be little to record. The minute books, beautifully handwritten until 1928, contain the core of this book, particularly for the early years. Thomas Fenwick, the first Secretary, set a high standard and no doubt was equally meticulous in the separate Competition book, now unfortunately lost. John Haslam's booklet, produced in 1950, contains important information on members and the winners of trophies.

Three of the later Secretaries have gone a step further and made direct contributions to the writing. Bobby Furber did the research and wrote the second chapter on Some Prominent Early Members and his research contributed substantially to the opening chapter. He also wrote from memory about the splendid opening game in 1961 against the Writers to the Signet GC and his memories and carefully preserved records fleshed out the post-war period. He also ensured the preservation of the minutes by paying for the rebinding of the five black leather-bound volumes. Peter Morley-Jacob wrote the first drafts about the matches against the lawyers from Scotland and East Anglia and has preserved material and photographs from his fellow Slaughter and May partners, Peter Marriage and Tommy Walmsley. James Furber has also contributed information, anecdotes and impetus, particularly in respect of his period as Secretary.

Jonathan Chalton did the early work of pulling together information for the book and is another who has the solicitor's tendency not to throw things away but carefully to put papers away in envelopes, all excellent for those coming later. He has gathered the details and written much of the passages on women and the Society, particularly the Ladies' Legal Golf Association, the Abady Cup and the early days. Most importantly, he has recorded LSGS in his photographs and these are the vast bulk of those included from the past 30 years.

The London Solicitors' GS owes a lot to a few law firms, including Slaughter and May when Peter Morley-Jacob was Secretary, where Peter's own secretary, Beryl Washington did much of the hard work. In recent years Farrer & Co. have supplied much support and Hazel McGuire, Adam Walker's secretary, typed and collated information in the appendices. Close readers will see that, as the book went to print in the summer of 2010, the Spring meeting results are included but not those for the Autumn where the winners may have a very long wait for the next history.

It has been helpful that other clubs and societies have been prompter than the Society in publishing books to celebrate their own centenaries. The most useful have been Bobby Furber's own history of Royal St George's GC, *A Course for Heroes* (1996), and the history of Walton Heath GC, *Heather and Heaven* (Pilley 2003), where Philip Truett did much of the research and he also commented on chapters of this book. The Walton Heath book contains much of the information of the extraordinary story of Lloyd George and Lord Riddell. The Aldeburgh GC history (1984) provided some of the information about Victor Longstaffe and the Aldeburgh connection. The books in the Aldeburgh library still contain pieces of paper in Bobby Furber's unmistakeable hand, evidence of his researches into the history of the Moles.

It is no surprise that most of the quotes in this book are from Bernard Darwin, and we are particularly lucky that he played against the Society for both Bar and Press and knew well, played against and wrote about, each of Riddell, Herbert Taylor, Vivian Pollock and Victor Longstaffe. There have been flashes of excitement, such as discovering that the great Harold Hilton had played against the Society. The quotes attributed to him come from his *My Golfing Reminiscences* (1907). Horace Hutchinson's comments on golfing societies and on Riddell are from his *Fifty Years of Golf* (1919). In both cases the quotes were written down from books which were the personal copies of Lord Riddell, now in the London Library in St James's Square as part of the bequest of Riddell's books. Mabel Stringer wrote about her involvement in ladies' golfing associations in her *Golfing Reminiscences* (1924) published, somewhat surprisingly, by Mills and Boon. For more on Harry Colt, *Creating Classics: The golf courses of Harry Colt* (Pugh and Lord 2008) should be read.

Many people have checked facts and provided information, particularly the informal committee of Jonathan Chalton, James Furber, Peter Morley-Jacob and Adam Walker, joined later by the sharp eyed Bill Richards. Michael Nathanson ensured a correct report of the Italian wartime escape of his father, Leslie. Keith Griffiths, Alasdair Loudon and others from the Writers to the Signet GC have been helpful on the Scottish passages. David Wybar helped on the East Anglian match and the match managers commented on their opposite number societies. Many others have supplied information, including Arfon Jones (who is rewarded by being placed ahead of Bobby Jones in the index). My wife, Jane Maxim, has read the proof, despite a lack of interest in golf.

A number of golf clubs are thanked for either directly providing assistance or doing so through their histories. They include Walton Heath, Royal St George's, Aldeburgh, Woking, Ashford Manor, Royal Mid-Surrey, Royal Ashdown Forest, Worplesdon, the R&A and the Honourable Company of Edinburgh Golfers. The centenary histories of golfing societies have helped including the Bar GS, Lloyd's GC and the Press GS.

The British Library's Newspapers collections at Colindale, with more than 693,000 bound volumes, is a great national asset and its proposed move to Yorkshire in 2012 will be a disaster for the London based researcher. The library was the source for a lot of the early information and the images from *The Illustrated Sporting and Dramatic News*, *Golf Illustrated*, *Golfing* and *World of Golf*. The London Library and the Signet Library (Felicity Cross) have also been good sources. Where there is no acknowledgement the photograph was probably taken by a member of the Society or by somebody with a camera primed by them, most by Tommy Walmsley, Peter Marriage and, more recently, Jonathan Chalton.

Richard Brazier painted the portrait of Bobby Furber as Field Marshall of Royal Blackheath and supplied the photograph on page 59. For other illustrations, thanks, and copyright is acknowledged as relevant, to *The Illustrated Sporting and Dramatic News* pages 1 (both), 2 (bottom), 7 (top), 9, 10 (both), 12 (bottom), 19 (top), 25, 26, 27 (top), 32, 35 (both), 39, 87 (both), 91 and 93, *Golf Illustrated* pages 3 (bottom), 7 (bottom), 14, 15, 16, 20 (both), 22 (top), 23, 24, 29, 30, 36 (left), 43, 96 (top) and 101, *Golfing* pages 4, 21 (top), 22 (bottom), 36 (right), 37, 42 (bottom), 44 and 94, *World of Golf* pages 31, 34 (right), 42 (top) and 49, *Newman's Guide to London Golf 1913* page 13, *Country Life* pages 5, 21 (bottom), 41, 47, 116 and cover back page (right), *Vanity Fair* page 3 (top), National Portrait Gallery, London pages 51 and 52, National Trust, Standen page 27 (bottom), Aldeburgh GC page 113, Ashford Manor GC pages 11, 12 (top) and 28, Royal Ashdown Forest GC page 55, Royal Mid-Surrey GC page 58, Royal St George's GC page 19 (bottom), Walton Heath GC pages 33 and 34 (left), Nic Brook page 100 and Ladies' Legal Golf Association pages 96 (bottom) and 98.

STEPHEN BARNARD

July 2010

CHAPTER ONE

Origins and Early Years
1904 to 1914

A BRISK DAY'S GOLF on one of England's great seaside courses, and not a meeting in an office, sparked the idea of the London Solicitors' Golfing Society. On Saturday 12th March 1904 at the Cinque Ports Golf Club (not then Royal), Deal, the recently formed Bar Golfing Society played its first match. The opponents were "a team of solicitors" raised by Francis E E Farebrother of Fladgate & Co and the proceedings were reported in *The Times* and *Golf Illustrated* and, with action photographs, in *The Illustrated Sporting and Dramatic News* and on the front cover of *Golfing*.

The Bar's team was led by Edward Marshall Hall, probably the best known advocate of the day. Mr Farebrother's team included Thomas Rawle (who was then Vice President of the Law Society), Charles Murray Smith, Thomas Fenwick and BEH Bircham.

The solicitors were victorious in both the singles and the afternoon foursomes but the match was played off handicap, so probably it should only be regarded as a friendly.

The success of the day prompted discussion among the solicitors on the train on the way back to London, for the following Wednesday a circular letter was sent to solicitors in London who were known to be golfers:

(left) Francis Farebrother (left) led the team of solicitors at Deal against the newly formed Bar Golfing Society. Edward Marshall Hall (right) led the Bar team

(right) W W Bury, sporting a stylish hat, plays a delicate shot for the solicitors up to the 6th green at Deal in 1904

The first page of the LSGS Minute Book

London
16th March 1904

Dear Sir,

It has been suggested that an Association or Club for Solicitors and Articled Clerks, who are Golfers, to be instituted on somewhat similar lines to the recently established Bar Golfing Society, would be popular among London Solicitors, as the Club could hold Meetings and Competitions amongst its own Members, and play Matches with kindred Associations.

The matter has been discussed by several Golfing Solicitors, and, as we understand you are a Golfer, we invite you to attend a Meeting which will be held at the Law Society's Hall, Chancery Lane (entrance in Bell Yard) on Thursday the 25th day of March instant, at 5 p.m. to discuss the matter, and if thought desirable to start the Club and appoint Officers etc.

Yours truly

Thomas Fenwick, the first Secretary and Treasurer, shows vigorous endeavour at Deal in 1904. His administrative abilities were probably superior to his golf

The letter was by signed by Farebrother, Murray Smith, Fenwick and Bircham and by six others including Vivian A Pollock and Herbert E Taylor, first class amateur golfers with + handicaps. The letter was short and to the point and yet still captures the purpose of the Society: it continues to the present day to have its own meetings and play matches against "kindred associations".

The meeting was "numerously attended" with Thomas Rawle in the chair. Thomas Fenwick, who had probably drafted the letter, explained the purpose of the meeting and a resolution was proposed: "That a Club or Society be formed among Solicitors and Articled Clerks who are Golfers for the purpose of holding Meetings and Competitions amongst its Members and of playing Matches with other Clubs or Societies, and that the subscription be 5/- per annum without entrance fee". The resolution was passed, with an amendment that the membership should be confined to solicitors and articled clerks practising or living within the Metropolitan area.

The name of "The London Solicitors Golfing Society" was adopted, never to be changed, although a more correct apostrophe is usually added, as it has been in versions of the Rules. Thomas Rawle was elected President and Charles Murray Smith Captain. Thomas Fenwick was elected as Joint Secretary with Herbert Taylor, and Fenwick also became Treasurer. The other members elected to constitute the first Committee were B E H Bircham, Francis Farebrother, H E Lawrence, Cyril Plummer, Ernest V Longstaffe and J E Tunnicliffe.

Thereafter, things moved swiftly.

A match play competition was under way before the end of April, with the Committee having fixed the handicaps – the 29 competitors being required to play off the rounds of the knock out on whatever course each pair agreed.

Thomas Fenwick was busy on the Rules of the Society and these were adopted, with just one small amendment, at the first annual meeting held on 18th May 1904 at the Café Royal, Regent Street. After the formal business, the members moved through to the Society's first dinner which was attended by 34 members and guests at a cost of 10/6d.

The first golf meeting was held at Mid-Surrey Golf Club (again not yet Royal) on Thursday 23rd June 1904, and immediately the Committee allowed for the inability of most members to keep going for a full round by giving additional prizes for nine holes out and in, the tradition of giving LSGS spoons as such prizes was introduced much later. Both of the Joint Sec-

Thomas Rawle, then Vice President of the Law Society, chaired the inaugural meeting and was the Society's first President

Hanger Hill Golf Club, Ealing in 1914. The Society's first Autumn meeting was played there in October 1904. The mature trees and course were swept away in the suburban boom of the 1920s

Herbert Taylor driving from the 11th tee at Royal St George's in the semi-final of the 1908 Amateur Championship. Darwin commented: "There is no better style to watch in the whole competition than his."

retaries were members but the meeting may have been initiated by Herbert Taylor who lived in Richmond with Mid-Surrey as one of his many clubs; a little later he held the course record with a 73.

So, after just three months, the London Solicitors' GS had adopted Rules at its first general meeting, the first match play competition was under way, the first dinner and the first golf meeting had been held and the Society already had 124 members.

Unfortunately, the results of the first meeting are not known as the Competition Book, kept separately from the Minute Book, has now been lost. Luckily, many of the Society's later matches and meetings were reported in *The Times* and elsewhere, including the 1904 Autumn meeting which took place at the Hanger Hill Club in Ealing, then on the "southern slopes of the high ground above the town" and now long since covered in houses. On a foggy October day Herbert Taylor won the scratch prize with an 83, which *The Times* commended as he was a late starter and played in the worst of the fog, but off +5 his net score was beaten by O S Vaughan (9) who had the second best gross score of 90 and by several others (even though handicaps had been limited by the Committee to 18).

This handicap limit was clearly not in place in 1905 when the President's cup at the Summer meeting was won by Leslie Blunt with a net 77 off 20 handicap. Niblick, the golf correspondent in *The Illustrated Sporting and Dramatic News*, commented rather archly: "One naturally welcomes the success of small handicap men, but at the same time one cannot deny to Mr Blunt the merit of having a game well up to his handicap".

Matches against the "kindred Associations" took longer to get going. Efforts

The London Solicitors' Golfing Society

in 1904 to arrange matches, notably against the Bar GS and the "medical profession", failed and there is no record of whether a "friendly" was played against Royal St George's members, which Charles Murray Smith, himself a prominent member, obtained permission to arrange.

The first recorded match in the LSGS history was against the Chartered Accountants' Golfing Society at Richmond Golf Club at Sudbrook Park on 30th March 1905, a "very sporting" course famous at the time for its golfers, again including Herbert Taylor, and where Bernard Darwin first hit the new rubber-cored Haskell ball. The Society was successful by 8-2, singles only being played. The Society's two best players, Herbert Taylor and Vivian Pollock, both played and the team was led by the Captain, Charles Murray Smith, who, unfortunately, was the only person to lose his game.

The Society also won its second match against the London Press GS at West Middlesex Golf Club on 4th May 1905, though the top LSGS player in the singles, R L Finnis, was beaten by Hal Ludlow, a well known artist and sculptor and the holder of the Welsh Amateur title.

Vivian Pollock: a great seaside course player

The first official match against the Bar took place at Royal St George's on 17th July 1905. This too was by singles only, perhaps because of the necessity of rail travel for many of those taking part. In these early days these fixtures were regarded seriously, were reported in the press, and much effort was put into fielding a good team and, in particular, to getting out the best players (sometimes called "cracks"). The Bar fielded a very strong team and won by 7-2 though, on this occasion, LSGS won the top match, Vivian Pollock beating the Bar's star player, Scottish international, H W Beveridge, by one hole. To do this Pollock had to go round in 76, equalling the amateur course record for Royal St George's. Herbert Taylor halved with Mansfield Hunter and the third famous Scottish player playing for the Bar, Ernley Blackwell, was too strong for Richard Dallmeyer.

The London Solicitors' GS was however successful in the matches against the Bar in the two following years, at Woking and Walton Heath. Bernard Darwin, the greatest golf correspondent of the first half of the 20th century and a very good player, played for the Bar on the second occasion: he had abandoned the solicitors' profession before the Society was formed and soon also ceased to practise at the Bar. But members of the Society were to continue to meet him regularly as the organiser of the London Press Golfing Society's team.

By 1905 the Society's activities had already taken shape: a Spring knock-out,

Summer and Autumn meetings, a dinner at the Cafe Royal and various matches against other societies. Early in that year it also acquired its first permanent cup, presented by George Riddell, a solicitor turned press magnate. Many more trophies were presented in the next few years as well as always generous prizes at the meetings, often cups or other pieces of silver to be won outright. Indeed, such was the money and array of prizes available, including in 1909 a pair of silver candlesticks, that the Committee gave anxious consideration to the possibility of loss of amateur status for a winner. The candlesticks however had a worthy winner in Stanley H Scott with a net 73 off 3 handicap. The presenter of the candlesticks was Thomas Markby who was related to Henry Markby, the model for the fictional solicitor Markby of whom Lady Bracknell approved in Oscar Wilde's *The Importance of Being Earnest*.

The Riddell Challenge Cup was initially played as a further match play knock-out, after qualification in a medal at the Summer meeting. In some years the four semi finalists were gathered together over a weekend to play the semi finals and the 36 hole final, often at Walton Heath. James Hall, who was Captain in 1911, won the cup for a second time in 1910 which prompted George Riddell that October to notify the Committee that anybody who won the cup three times could keep it and he would provide a new and "more handsome" cup to replace it. In the event, this did not happen when it was eventually won for a third time by Bertie Trayton Kenward in 1924 and the original cup continued as a prize; as it is to this day, albeit now in a different competition at the Spring meeting.

These match play events appear usually to have been completed on time without any need for rulings by the Committee: halcyon days indeed when work did not unduly interfere with pleasure, or perhaps when the solicitor could rely on his managing clerk to do the bulk of the work. The Society was also increasing in popularity: in the six years to 1910, at every general meeting there was a proud announcement of another increase in numbers.

The Summer meetings of the Society from 1905 until the war were all held at Ashford Manor Golf Club, where the great amateur golfer Harold H Hilton lived and was, for a while, Secretary. Beveridge and Finnis were members there as was Henry Mossop, who arranged not only for the meetings to be held on a Saturday, but also to be free of charge. LSGS reciprocated with various gifts to the Club, including a barometer, a notice board and a clock. Things were done on a permanent basis in those days, and the barometer and the clock are still at Ashford Manor, on display and working. The Autumn meetings were held midweek at various clubs, always with a railway station nearby (this was still the age of the train) and usually, again, with the courtesy of the course. The meetings were sometimes followed by a dinner, with the minutes noting a requirement for hot dishes: one club was rejected on this basis. These meetings were well

Herbert Taylor on the 6th green at Royal St George's in the final of the Amateur in 1908 when, sadly, his putting, as well as the rest of his game, deserted him

Victor Longstaffe (right) and Harold Hilton crossing the bridge at the 3rd at Stoke Poges while playing in the Golf Illustrated Gold Vase in June 1911. Victor Longstaffe was one of the Society's best early players and a co-founder that year of the Moles. Harold Hilton had won the Amateur two weeks before and was to win the US Amateur later in the year. Hilton is the best player ever to have played against the Society. On the day, Herbert Taylor did better than either of them with a fine 148 (75+73)

attended; often between 70 to 80 members, playing singles in the mornings and, usually, foursomes in the afternoons.

The Society had, from the beginning, golfing quality as well as quantity amongst its members. In *Nisbet's Golf Year Book* for 1911, six LSGS members are listed in the *Who's Who of the World's Leading Amateur Golfers*. In the early days there were probably more than ten members with handicaps of scratch or better, although scratch was a more fluid concept before the introduction of standard scratch scoring. Herbert Taylor had the most impressive record, reaching the final of the Amateur Championship at Royal St George's in 1908, and playing for England in 1911. During the 1908 Amateur, Bernard Darwin commented that there was "no better style to watch in the whole competition than his". Vivian Pollock also played for England and could be brilliant at times as well as powerful. On 9th April 1904, just a couple of weeks after the formation of the Society, Pollock had a 70 at Felixstowe in a major amateur event, breaking the amateur course record by seven shots and four shots less than the professional record. But he did not shake off the field and after three rounds was tied with Herbert Taylor and one other on 249.

Another excellent player in the early days was Victor Longstaffe who broke the course record at Aldeburgh with a 72 in 1907, was Captain of Golf at Cambridge the next year and co-founder of the Moles in 1911. One of Longstaffe's opponents in the Oxford team was Denys Finch Hatton, later to emigrate to Kenya and famously become the lover of Karen Blixen, as described in her book *Out of Africa*. Many years later, in the film of the same name, he was played by Robert Redford with a complete disregard as to how an Englishman of that era would look, behave and speak.

The closest Taylor, Pollock and Longstaffe as a group came to representative honour was perhaps in 1911 when they all played at Stoke Poges for a very strong team of Gentlemen against a team of Ladies, where five of the 12 Gentlemen had played in the final of the Amateur. Niblick assumed it was "a pleasant and cheery day's amusement, without the introduction of the too serious side of golf".

The Society got out its best players for the top matches, particularly against the Bar, the Stock Exchange and the London Press. The matches against the Press seem to have been especially competitive, and in 1906 the Press fielded Harold Hilton, the best player ever to have played against the Society. He had been Open Champion in 1892 and 1897, had won the Amateur Championship in successive years (1900 and 1901) after previously losing three times in the final, and was then one of the best players in the world, amateur or professional. He remains the last British amateur to win the Open. He was perhaps better as a "scoreman" rather than a match player, with a handicap of +10 in 1900. In 1911 he was to achieve the extraordinary feat of winning both the Amateur and the US Amateur and was only one shot behind Harry Vardon, the winner, in that year's Open at Royal St George's, having gone out in 33 in the final round only to fade to a 76. The 1911 Open also saw a fine performance from Herbert Taylor who was the second leading amateur after Hilton and his 73 in the second round was better than any of the rounds of Hilton or Vardon. Unfortunately, his opening score of 83 meant he was never in contention in one of the tightest of all Opens.

On his way to the first tee for his 1906 match at Walton Heath, Hilton

The Ladies v Gentlemen game at Stoke Poges in 1911. Taylor is the small figure on the left and Pollock appears to be above Harold Hilton's "The same old fling". Longstaffe also played in the very strong Gentlemen's team. The drawing is by Harry Rountree who was later captain of the London Press GS

probably called in to see James Braid, the club professional, who had battled with Hilton for the Open in 1897 on Hilton's home course, Hoylake, which was "hard and burnt, and in consequence was as keen as a skating rink", just as it was 109 years later for Tiger Woods in the 2006 Open. In those days 36 holes were played on each of the two days of the Championship and the leaders were not grouped together. Hilton had finished early, at which point Braid was only on the 8th and Hilton had to wait as Braid played well over the back nine, knowing he had to come back in 37 to equal Hilton's score. Hilton tried to distract himself by playing billiards in the clubhouse but went out to watch Braid play

The 2nd green of the newly opened Walton Heath in 1904. The almost complete absence of trees meant there was little protection against the wind and rain

Bernard Darwin at Lytham in 1904

the last. Braid needed a three on the 18th to tie and Hilton said "in James Braid's long career he has probably seldom hit a better shot than that second of his to this last hole in 1897; it was never off the pin". Fortunately for Hilton, it missed the hole by a foot and rolled on for 20 feet on the baked green and Braid just missed the putt back on the left, giving Hilton the Championship. James Braid would have been too discreet to remind Hilton that he had received £40 of plate as an amateur for winning the Open while Braid, in second place and the leading professional, had only received a cash prize of £20.

When Hilton walked across to the first tee the weather conditions were very different for his match that day against the Society's Vivian Pollock (Herbert Taylor was playing in the second match). *The Times* reported that strong wind and heavy rain made Walton Heath very difficult, although this would not have stopped Hilton chain smoking cigarettes throughout his round. But Pollock was up for the challenge and won three holes in a row to be one up on Hilton after 11 holes, only for Hilton to re-impose himself and win 2 and 1. The Society, however, came through 4 ¾ -2 ½ overall.

Some of the competitiveness in the Press matches may have been due to the influence of George Riddell who, in the early days, played for the Press rather than London Solicitors' GS. He also captained both societies; the Press in 1907 and LSGS in 1910.

In 1910, the year of his captaincy, Riddell ensured the Society fielded possibly

the strongest team in its history against the London Press and won 10 – 2, although Bernard Darwin won both his games for the Press. The three top players, Taylor, Pollock and Longstaffe, all played. The fourth player, Maurice Copland, also better than scratch, was the holder of the course record at Stanmore with a 75 and won two rounds in the Amateur Championship in 1912 before losing to Bernard Darwin at the 19th. A H O'Bryen-Taylor (1 handicap), K M Beaumont (scratch), H R I Dyne and James Hall (3) made up the rest of the team. K M Beaumont and James Hall were Society regulars and low handicap prize-winners for many years and Beaumont was good enough to beat Harold Beveridge in the 1920 match against the Bar. As Taylor, Pollock and Longstaffe were probably each +3, +4 or +5, the combined average handicap of the Society's team would have been better than scratch: the game itself was played level. Bernard Darwin agreed with the strength of the side in his comments on the match in *Country Life*. After reviewing, as usual, his own performance in the third person, he noted "Mr Longstaffe, Mr Copland and Mr O'Brien-Taylor all played well for the Solicitors, who were altogether far too strong a side".

In March 1906 the Society played the Cricketers, although *The Times* reported them as G L Jessop's Team. Gilbert Jessop was one of the top sporting stars of the age, and in 1902 had destroyed the Australians at the Oval with one of the most celebrated innings of all. Coming in at 48 for 5, on a tricky wicket and with England needing 263 to win, Jessop scored the fastest Test century off just 75 balls, a record that was to stand for many years. This great innings enabled England to struggle home with the last pair, Hirst and Rhodes, at the crease. Jessop's hitting drew crowds wherever Gloucestershire or England were

Gilbert Jessop led a team of Cricketers against LSGS in 1906. He remains the only man to have hit a ball over the Pavilion at Lord's

playing and he once hit a ball over the Pavilion at Lord's. Although the Cricketers had three scratch players, Jessop himself played off 6, although he was down to scratch by 1911. Perhaps he was similar to W G Grace as described by James Braid: powerful with the wood but potentially fallible with the iron.

Jessop's new-found obsession with golf may have affected his cricket. In the opening Test against Australia at Trent Bridge the previous year he had been bowled first ball: "My only stroke was more reminiscent of an iron shot than any stroke known to careful students of batsmanship". He was dropped for the rest of the series.

We can still marvel at Jessop's mighty hit at Lords: he remains the only person to have cleared the Pavilion. This is because, in cricket, both bat and ball remain basically the same as they were a century ago. Any equivalent hit in golf would now be meaningless because of changes to both club and ball, particularly following the introduction of hollow metal woods, which have rendered many fine old courses obsolete for the modern player and reduced the terror of the "carry", a feature of the Edwardian game. If only the golf authorities had been as tough over hollow metal woods and changes to the ball as the cricket umpires had been in banning Dennis Lillee's aluminium bat.

The Edwardian era was the golden age for the golfing society or association. Many were founded about the same time as LSGS. Lloyd's Golf Club had led the way in 1894, followed by the Chartered Accountants GS in 1898. Of the other

The 8th green at Rye (now the 5th) in 1904 - an early example of Harry Colt's eye for placing short hole greens on top of dunes and hummocks

London Corn Exchange Golfing Society.

Annual subscription, 5s.
Hon. Secretary : Mr. H. BAKER MUNTON, 34, Mark Lane, E.C.
Telephone : Avenue, 4,180.

London Discount Market Golfing Society.

Hon. Secretary : Mr. S. M. LIGHTON, National Discount Co., Cornhill, E.C.
Telephone : Avenue, 1,484.

London Metal Exchange Golfing Association.

This Association is connected with the London Metal Exchange, has no course of its own, and was instituted in 1905.
The Hon. Secretary is Mr. MALCOLM BOWLEY, 46, Fenchurch Street, E.C.
Telephone : Avenue, 995.

The London Municipal Golfing Society.

This Society consists of present and past members and officers of Local Government Bodies in the area of greater London. It was founded in 1898. The annual subscription is 5s., and there is also an entrance fee of 5s. Competitions and matches are held in connection with the Society.
The President for 1912 was the Right Hon. the Lord CHEYLESMORE, 16, Prince's Gate, S.W.
The Captain, Mr. PERCY G. GATES, M.A., 5, Manson Place, S. Kensington, S.W.
The Hon. Secretaries are Mr. FRANCIS ROBINSON, Town Hall, Greenwich, S.E., and Mr. T. APLIN MARSH (Treasurer), 129, Fulham Palace Road, Hammersmith, W.

London Press Golfing Society.

This Society exists for the use of journalists and others connected with the Press.
Membership.—There are now 140 members, who pay an entrance fee of 10s. and an annual subscription of 5s.
The chief Club Events are the Spring Meetings for the Society's Prizes, the Summer Meeting for the Captain's Prize, and the Autumn Meeting for the Challenge Cup; also matches against kindred societies.

The Hon. Secretary is Mr. S. W. FOWLER DIXON, 2, Whitefriars Street, London, E.C.
The Captain, Mr. HARRY ROUNTREE, Dormer's Wells, Southall.
Telephone : (Hon. Secretary), Holborn, 2,375 (3 lines).

London Scottish Golf Club.

This club has joint use of the course on Wimbledon Common, and there is therefore no Sunday play. It is 2 miles from Wimbledon, 2 from Putney (L. and S.W.R.), and just over 1 mile from Southfields on the District R.
Membership.—250. Entrance fees £4 4s. and £2 2s. and an annual subscription of £3 3s.
Professional : D. WILSON, London Scottish Golf Club, Wimbledon, S.W.
Hon. Secretary : Col. H. WALKER, London Scottish Golf Club, Wimbledon Common, S.W.
Telephone : Putney, 135.

The London Solicitors' Golfing Society.

This Society has no course belonging to it, but plays on the various courses in the Metropolitan district.
Membership.—There is no entrance fee, but an annual subscription of 5s., due on February 1st, which can be compounded by a payment of £2 after payment of four subscriptions, or of £3 otherwise. There is no limit to the membership, and there are 200 members at present. The Summer and Autumn Meetings, the Spring Tournament, and matches with other societies and clubs are all in the calendar.
The Hon. Secretary is Mr. T. C. FENWICK, 16, Berners' Street, W.
The Captain is Mr. HENRY MOSSOP, 11, Lincoln's Inn Fields, W.C.

London Stock Exchange Golfing Society.

This Society is open to any member of the Stock Exchange, and all clerks admitted to the House.
Membership.—There are about 400 members who pay no fixed entrance fee or subscription. Competitions are held at various times and matches played against other golfing societies on courses lent for the occasion.
The Joint Hon. Secretaries and Treasurers are Mr. W. BRANDER, jun., 5, Draper's Gardens, Throgmorton Street, E.C., and Mr. C. G. TUNKS, Stock Exchange, E.C.

LSGS and other London golfing societies in Newman's Guide to London Golf 1913, which, in the age of the train, included the train timetables for all the London golf clubs

societies with fixtures with LSGS, the Bar GS was founded in 1903, the London Press GS, George Edwardes GS (acting and stage) and the Baltic Exchange GS in 1904, the London Stock Exchange GS in 1905 and the Chartered Surveyors GS and the Engineers GS in 1907. The Society was closely involved in the formation of the Ladies' Legal Golf Association in 1913 and in that year gave a rose bowl as a prize to the Association and also played its first match against the ladies.

Horace Hutchinson noted that these were the years of the formation of the "wandering teams" without a green: "There were the Bar Golfing Society, the Solicitors', the Army – every self-respecting profession had to have its Golfing Society".

By 1907 the Society already had eight matches in place, beating the Press and the Bar, losing to the Chartered Accountants, the Chartered Surveyors, Lloyd's, the Engineers and Sundridge Park and halving with the Stock Exchange. Some of these matches would have been friendlies, unlike the representative matches against the Press, the Bar and the Stock Exchange. Extraordinarily, all of these matches, apart from the Engineers and Sundridge Park, were still being played one hundred years later. Indeed, apart from the matches against teams of solicitors from Scotland, East Anglia and Ireland, all of the Society's 21st century matches, other than the Wine Trade, have their origins before the First World War.

Initially it was easy for the newly formed societies and associations to find

Vivian Pollock (sitting centre right) in the England team in 1908. Two other members of the team had also trained as solicitors. Bernard Darwin (sitting left) was embarking on his golf writing career, after a spell at the Bar, and Harry Colt (standing behind Darwin) was shortly to take up golf course architecture on a full time basis. Sitting between Pollock and Darwin is John Ball, eight times Amateur Champion and the first Englishman and the first amateur to win the Open

golf courses on which to play, usually with the courtesy of the course, as many golf clubs were in the process of being built and they were looking to establish themselves. As this became more difficult, there was talk in 1912 and 1913 of the societies themselves laying out their own course for their own exclusive use. George Edwardes was in the lead and plans were developed for the proposal, with the capital to be raised for the new course estimated at £12,000. The matter was discussed at the Society's annual general meeting in 1913 but the Committee was sceptical and, in the event, the outbreak of the First World War in 1914 brought an end to the plans.

A little earlier the Committee had looked into forming some sort of permanent arrangement at Littlestone involving the payment of a subscription but this was turned down, partly on the advice of the expert Herbert Taylor who was concerned at the likely effect of discouraging the Society from playing elsewhere. Ever since, the Society has enjoyed the facilities of a number of courses, often involving close links over many years with a number of clubs including Royal St George's, Walton Heath, Woking, Aldeburgh, Worplesdon, Royal Ashdown Forest and Royal Wimbledon.

If the London Solicitors' GS had been formed a decade earlier it might have

been able to claim a direct connection with the design or redesign of many of the courses played on by the Society over the years, including Rye, Muirfield, Sunningdale, Wentworth, Royal Wimbledon, St George's Hill, Swinley Forest and Aldeburgh. The great golf course architect Harry Colt had a hand in all of these courses. In 1894 he was practising as a solicitor and had just become a partner in Sayer and Colt of Hastings, having been Captain of golf at Cambridge in 1890, and was about to engage on his first golf course project, the laying out of Rye, one of the great seaside courses. No doubt the Society would have stretched the London qualification to admit him as a member as it has done for others from time to time. By 1900, Harry Colt was secretary of Sunningdale and in 1913 took up golf course architecture on a full time basis, with other later masterpieces to include Royal Portrush and Pine Valley.

Many golfing solicitors have fancied trying their hand at golf course architecture: Harry Colt actually did so, and supremely well.

Harry Colt was also a good enough golfer to be selected to play for England against Scotland in 1908 at Sandwich alongside the Society's Vivian Pollock, in the week Old Tom Morris died. Unfortunately they both lost their matches on the 35th green, although Pollock "had a very fine match, with good play on both sides". In the Amateur Championship, held immediately after the international, Colt reached the quarter finals, losing to Herbert Taylor who played a spectacular bunker shot on the 19th followed by a four yard putt to win. The accolade for the best solicitor golfer however perhaps belongs to a much more recent player, Peter McEvoy, the amateur champion of the 1970s and 80s.

In the early years, in addition to matches against societies, LSGS also played some matches against golf clubs with their own courses, notably Burhill and

Sir George Riddell portrayed by
Charles Ambrose in 1914

the Automobile Club (later the RAC) at Woodcote Park. Such was the vibrancy of the Society in its first decade that in February 1913 Robson Sadler reported that he was taking a team from the Society over to Dublin to play against the Dublin Solicitors at Whitsuntide. It is not known whether he was successful: but if he was it would have been the Society's earliest overseas expedition by many years. It would take the Society another 93 years to play golf again in Ireland.

This was a well ordered age with the time and money for leisure and golf: the product of almost a century of the Pax Britannica, in place since the Battle of Waterloo in 1815. There is an intriguing glimpse in the minutes. James Beale, twice President of the London Solicitors' GS in the early years and later to be President of the Law Society, had taken an extended holiday to India. In March 1907 a letter to the Society from him, posted from Agra, is reproduced in full, dealing in the main with the presentation of a piece of Kashmiri silverware, sent with the letter, to be played for at a Society meeting. It is comforting to know that, over a hundred years ago, English tourists were already being accosted outside the Taj Mahal by Kashmiri traders. It is probably uncharitable to think that his wife may have suggested immediately posting the silverware straight off to the Society.

Later in the letter he says: "I am here for the great function of the reception of the Amir of Afghanistan by the Viceroy [of India]. There are great and gorgeous shows every day, finishing up with a big review of 30,000 troops on Saturday".

At this time the British Raj was at its height, as were the intrigues surrounding Afghanistan which was central to the Great Game between Britain and Russia. The use of 30,000 troops for a display was surely more than ceremonial: it must also have been intended as a demonstration of strength to the watching Amir of Afghanistan. If so, it did not have the desired effect, as following the Third Afghan War in 1919 British influence in Afghanistan came to an end; although British troops were to return again in 2001, this time as an ally of another imperial power.

The Society's dinners were held every year until the First World War at the Cafe Royal, with increasing numbers attending. The Cafe Royal closed in 2008 but in the 1900s it was in its pomp, with plush banquettes and ornate mirrors and mahogany woodwork; just a few years earlier it had been a favourite dining place for the Oscar Wilde set. In later years there were musical entertainments after the dinner, often paid for by Sir George Riddell, after he became Captain in 1910 and then President in 1911. In 1914 the Committee itself provided the entertainment – surely beyond the call of duty and perhaps the ability of the Committee members involved – and C V Young and C E Stredwick performed. The minutes intriguingly refer to "Mr C E Stredwick … who played a flute solo and whose daughter also kindly gave her services". There is no elaboration as to the nature of the services given by Mr Stredwick's daughter.

Francis Ouimet had been invited to the 1914 dinner but was unable to attend and so missed the excitement of the flute solo and other services provided by the Stredwick family. Ouimet had achieved enormous fame following his victory, as a young amateur, in the US Open at Brookline the previous year after a play off against Harry Vardon and Ted Ray; perhaps one of the most unexpected wins in golfing history. He was probably then the most celebrated amateur golfer in the world and, at the time of the dinner, had crossed the Atlantic, with other Americans including Jerome Travers (four times US Amateur champion), to try and win the Amateur Championship on its first return to Royal St George's since LSGS's Herbert Taylor had been runner-up in 1908. Bernard Darwin regarded this expedition as the start of what became American dominance between the wars, but he thought Jerome Travers would be the main threat. In the event, the fancied players fell away early on and the Championship was won by J L C Jenkins from Troon.

What a time to have been a Society member: internationals in the team, golf against Harold Hilton, Bernard Darwin and Gilbert Jessop, echoes of Oscar Wilde and dinner invitations to Francis Ouimet. Luckily, throughout this stimulating period for golf, the Society was being quietly and effectively run by Thomas Fenwick from his offices at 16 Berners Street, W1, where the Committee meetings were held. The London Solicitors' Golfing Society had been well founded.

CHAPTER TWO

Some Prominent Early Members

F R Furber

T HIS WRITER MUST start this tentative account with a heart-felt apology for his lack of foresight, as a new member of the London Solicitors' Golfing Society, sixty years ago. This failure was brought to his notice by a small booklet entitled *The London Solicitors' Golfing Society 1949–50*. It contains a list of the members of the Society in early 1950, following a determined effort by the Hon. Secretary and the Committee to put the Society back on its pre-war footing by means of a successful recruiting campaign.

Surprisingly, this list contains no less than thirty-nine members elected before the outbreak of war in 1914: of these, thirty were pre-1910 and only nine elected in the remaining five years – an indication of the tragic loss of young lives on the battlefield.

C G Armstrong of 6 Coleman Street is asterixed as an "Original Member" – and there are four more who joined in 1904. "1930" appears against the name of J R (Jack) Mason, the famous Winchester, Kent and England cricketer, though the Minute Book shows that he was originally elected at the first Committee meeting in April 1904 but resigned a couple of years later – probably having little time to play golf during the summer months.

For a future Secretary of the Society, interested in golf history, to have failed to take the opportunity to canvass these survivors of Edwardian golf for memories is ample cause for apology. It also explains the inadequacies in the following portraits of members selected, for one reason or another, as "prominent". The overall impression is of an era of ample means, lots of leisure and a passion for golf.

Prominence cannot be denied to Francis Edward Essington Farebrother as organiser of the team of London solicitors who engaged in the first match of the Bar Golfing Society at Deal, described in the first chapter, which preceded the formation of LSGS. The records show that he was admitted as a solicitor in 1870, became a partner in Fladgate & Co in 1876 and by 1904 was second in the firm to William Fladgate. The firm's office was then at No. 2 Craig's Court, off the top end of Whitehall: it later moved to a handsome building at the west end of Pall Mall.

The action photograph of Farebrother does not suggest great golfing skill but his enthusiasm for the game is evidenced by his membership of the Mid-Surrey Club and at West Herts – both excellent parkland courses, frequented by many of the best players around London.

Francis Farebrother served on the Society's first Committee but his name does not appear in the Minute Book after February 1905. He died at a ripe old age in 1932.

Francis Farebrother in action at Deal against the Bar

The first Captain of the Society is the obvious next choice for mention. Of Charles Murray Smith rather more has been discovered. He was a member of Farebrother's team at Deal and also a signatory of the letter to golfing solicitors circulated the following week. The affection and respect in which he was held was demonstrated by his re-election as Captain in the succeeding two years, and in the following year (1907) he served as President. No other Captain of the Society has served for three years, save for the "caretaker" Captains during the two World Wars. Murray Smith also had the distinction of leading the Society to victory in its first match – which was against the Chartered Accountants' Golfing Society.

He was born in 1860 and started to play golf in 1869, at St Andrews. His family were certainly Scottish in origin. Educated at Eton and Oxford, he was admitted as a solicitor in 1886 and joined a City firm in Suffolk Lane, off Cannon Street. By 1904 this was known by the name of its three partners – Kekewich, Smith and Kaye – the first named being the son of the well known judge.

Murray Smith was a founder member of St George's in 1887: the following year he joined the Royal & Ancient. He was to become Captain of Royal St George's in 1910 and Honorary Treasurer there from 1916 until his death in 1927. He was also a member of Reigate Heath, Royal Wimbledon, New Zealand and Prince's (Sandwich). His lowest handicap was 2 and his proudest golfing moments included the two occasions on which he was a winner of the Sidgwick Foursomes Challenge Cup at Royal St George's – a trophy presented to the club by Edward Sidgwick (another original member of LSGS) which is played for as the principal event of the club's Easter Meeting.

Charles Murray Smith was the Society's first captain. This photograph hangs in the main corridor of Royal St George's where he was also captain and later treasurer

Until the outbreak of war in 1914 called a halt to the Society's activities, the "headquarters" of LSGS were the offices of Messrs. Dod, Longstaffe and Fenwick at 16 Berners Street, W1 and the Co–Hon Secretary and the Treasurer throughout that period was Thomas Collingwood Fenwick of that firm. He was duly rewarded in 1914 with Honorary Membership of the Society. His senior partner, Ernest Victor Longstaffe, served on the Committee and was Captain in 1909. JL Longstaffe, Ernest's father, was a member and in 1909 a third, Ernest's

son Victor, became the first articled clerk to serve on the Committee: we think this can be attributed to his handicap of +2 and his Captaincy of Cambridge golf in 1907 rather than to nepotism.

From the first Minute Book, one can deduce that Mr Fenwick was a meticulous lawyer for only three corrections were found necessary to be made to the hand-written minutes as approved at each succeeding meeting. He was admitted a solicitor in 1877 – five years before Ernest Longstaffe. They were both early members of Aldeburgh (founded in 1884), where they had country houses and where Ernest Longstaffe had already been Captain in 1900.

"Fenwick" and "Collingwood" are suggestive of roots in Northumberland and if that is right, one can hazard a guess that Alnmouth – one of only half-a-dozen golf clubs in England in his boyhood – was his golfing *alma mater*. If so, he failed to benefit from an early start because his handicap in later life varied between 16 and 18. But no-one would question his enthusiasm.

In view of the Society's popular annual match at Aldeburgh against the East Anglian solicitors which was instituted in the mid 1970s, it is worthy of note that Fenwick was Captain of Aldeburgh in 1910 and arranged matches between LSGS and Aldeburgh, at Aldeburgh, in 1911 and 1913, the Society winning the first by a single point and the second being halved.

(top) Thomas Fenwick sitting (right) with JL Longstaffe (the father of Ernest Longstaffe) in the 1920s with Victor Longstaffe standing behind

(bottom) Ernest Longstaffe photographing Mabel Potterton on the 1st tee at Aldeburgh on a snowy day in January 1911. The gorse bushes had yet to grow

Thomas Fenwick's funeral was reported in *The Times* of 2nd March 1934: it was attended by "office and household staff" but his partner Ernest Longstaffe had died in 1919 and son Victor had not returned to the firm after wartime service in the RFC and RAF. Instead, he went into the wine-trade and throughout the 1920s welcomed golfing friends who dropped in for a drink with him at Denham's in Piccadilly (now part of Cordings). Victor and his wife were at the funeral and doubtless Thomas Fenwick was remembered by all his surviving contemporaries in the Society which owes him so much.

The Honorary Co-Secretary of LSGS until his resignation in 1910 was Herbert Edward Taylor, a solicitor in sole practice in Temple Chambers. Compared with Thomas Fenwick, his contribution to the organisation of the Society was slight, consisting mainly in the arranging of certain matches, notably against the Bar. His reputation as one of the leading London golfers, a member of many golf clubs and a lowest handicap of +5 must have added to the standing of LSGS among the rapidly increasing number of golfing societies in the Metropolis.

Herbert Taylor was born in 1869, educated at Wellington and admitted solicitor in 1894. His name was first associated with the Richmond Golf Club in Sudbrook Park, where he was the winner of countless scratch medals and prizes and he held the course record with a 71. It would seem that he applied himself to law for some years but after 1899, when he made his first appearance in the Amateur Championship, his absences from Temple Chamber could only have been increasingly frequent in view of press reports of his appearance (and successes) at golfing events not only in and around London, but also at St Andrews, North Berwick and, further afield, at Pau, Biarritz and the Riviera. At Sunningdale he won the scratch Gold Medal in five successive years, 1909–1913; at the R&A he was to win seven medals between 1912 and 1935, including the George Glennie medal, for the best scratch score at the Spring and Autumn Meetings, twice. In 1911, he played for England against Scotland at Royal St George's, where twenty-two years later he was a member of the British Seniors team, with Bernard Darwin, which heavily defeated both the American and Canadian Seniors.

From 1899 to 1937 he only missed appearing in five Amateur Championships (1925, 26 and 28 and 1932 and 33) and won a total of thirty-seven matches.

His best years were 1909, at Muirfield, when he was beaten in the fifth round by Bernard Darwin, and in 1912 at Westward Ho! when he turned the tables on Darwin, also in the fifth round, but then lost to Angus Hambro. After the War he reached the fifth round again, in 1923 at Deal. But his greatest achievement was at Royal St George's in 1908 when he reached the final, after a victory over the favourite, John Graham of Hoylake. The other finalist was an Old Rugbeian Yorkshireman called E A Lassen, a less stylish player than Taylor, though, on this occasion at least, possessed of more stamina and a steadier nerve. One down after eighteen holes, Taylor's game fell away after lunch (much as other LSGS golfers' games would

(top) Victor Longstaffe as a Cambridge player in 1908: "an extremely neat and attractive style"

(bottom) Herbert Taylor was the Society's best card and pencil player

Herbert Taylor bunkered in the final of the 1908 Amateur

Herbert Taylor playing from the 16th tee at Royal St George's in the morning of the final of the Amateur. Like many later LSGS players he faded after lunch

do in years to come) and he lost by what used to be called a "dog's licence", i.e. 7 and 6. His swansong in the Championship was not to come until 1937, again at Royal St George's, when he was sixty-seven or sixty-eight but still possessing the scratch handicap necessary for entry. He won his first round match against a fellow Sunningdale member and then took the Essex County Champion to the last hole before making his final bow.

His 1908 portrait by Charles Ambrose suggests a somewhat aloof character: elsewhere it is said that he was a good, though exacting, foursomes partner. Bernard Darwin, who knew him well, wrote that "the devil himself would not know what is in the mind of Mr. Taylor while the most nervous of partners is attacking the most critical of putts". He also referred to Taylor's vast collection of clubs, reputed to be more than 1,500, and his heavily laden caddie – but he considered that "for an easy and graceful swing, Taylor's is hard to beat ... achieving a long ball with no apparent effort".

Herbert Taylor died in 1945, when shortage of newsprint denied us an obituary, so the writer can say no more about this remarkable golfer.

Although the London Solicitors' Golfing Society could field nearly a dozen members in those early days with handicaps of better than scratch, there was only one other member than Taylor, however, who was rated, at one club or another, as low as +5. That was a large young man named Vivian Arthur Pollock, who we can imagine, walked to the Society's inaugural meeting at the Law Society's Hall from his father's office at 6 Lincoln's Inn Fields in particularly good spirits, having cleared the hurdle of the Solicitors' Final Examination a week or two earlier.

Bernard Darwin's description of his play is in sharp contrast to H E Taylor's, "Mr Pollock", he wrote in 1908, "hits the ball so hard and so far ... indeed, seems to hurl himself upon it in a sort of divine frenzy, then pursues it at a gait that would ensure his disqualification in a walking race".

"Vi" Pollock, as he was known in the golfing world, learnt to play his golf as Darwin had done, on the challenging nine-hole course beside the estuary at Felixstowe – vividly described in Darwin's *Golf Courses of Great Britain*, but since much eroded by the sea.

Vivian Pollock

He was a member of the large and distinguished legal, military and medical family descended from David Pollock of Charing Cross, saddler to King George III. By 1904, he was a member of Royal St George's, of the R&A, Royal Wimbledon and, of course, Felixstowe. It was from the last named club that he had entered the Amateur Championships of 1900 and 1902.

Pollock was elected to the LSGS Committee in 1906 and that year organised the Society's first visit to Walton Heath Golf Club, to play its second match against the London Press Golfing Society when he played Harold Hilton. His greatest achievements for LSGS were his single victories, playing No. 1, in the first two matches against the Bar Golfing Society. In 1905, at Royal St George's he had to hole the course in 76 strokes to beat Harold Beveridge by one hole: the following year, at Woking, he won at the 17th against Mansfield Hunter, another formidable Scottish golfer.

Pollock's record in the Amateur Championship does not match Herbert Taylor's. He won sixteen matches in thirteen appearances, reaching the fifth round in 1902, (when the rubber-cored Haskell ball was introduced), to be beaten by Charles Hutchings of the home club, Hoylake, who went on to become, at 53, the then oldest champion. In 1904, he lost by 1 hole in the fourth round to Robert Harris – future Champion and Walker Cup Captain. The following year he was beaten in the fourth round by Charlie Dick – one of the great Hoylake golfers. He also reached the fourth round in 1921 at St Andrews: thereafter he only entered the Championship when it was at Sandwich or St Andrews, but he

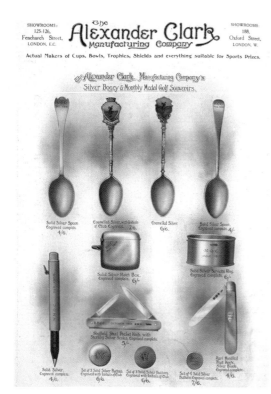

The Edwardians liked silver trophies - advertisements for spoons and cups were common. Some of the spoons are for Walton Heath and the buttons for Aldeburgh

failed to win another match. His final appearance was at St Andrews in 1930.

On the plus side of his golfing account are his performances in the R&A Autumn meeting of 1907 when he won the Royal Medal with the outstanding score of 74 and the match-play vase off +1. He was fortunate that Horace Hutchinson, twice Amateur Champion and golf correspondent for *Country Life*, was playing in the group ahead of him in the medal and watched as Pollock's ball always finished near the hole. The following week's edition noted, "The 74 ... was the result of perfect golf ... probably the finest ever returned, under any circumstances, for this medal". In consequence, one can readily conclude, he was chosen in 1908 to play in the international match against Scotland which then preceded the Amateur Championship and it was in that same Championship, at Royal St George's, that he gave his best performance in match play. He won his first match by 6 and 4; in the second round he had the temerity to beat the holder, the mighty John Ball, by 6 and 5. He succumbed, in the fifth round, again to Charles Dick – though at the 20th hole. Had it gone the other way, perhaps it might have been an exclusively LSGS final against Herbert Taylor.

It is surprising that the minutes of the next LSGS Committee meeting after the Championship contain no vote of congratulations to the Committee members Taylor and Pollock. Instead, Herbert Taylor only appears on the record of that meeting as proposing that the Society's Autumn meeting be held at Worplesdon (shortly to be opened to play). Had Vivian Pollock been present, he would surely have seconded the motion, as he, as well as Taylor, was about to add Worplesdon to his list of club memberships.

Our next "prominent member", George Allardice Riddell, was elected to the Society in July 1904: he was then thirty-nine years old, a recent convert to golf and just retired from a highly successful solicitor's practice to become Chairman of the *News of the World* which he had acquired for clients, the Carr family of Cardiff, a few years previously.

He was an original member of Walton Heath Golf Club, whose magnificent course was opened for play in May 1904. Golf, politics and the continuing amassing of a large fortune were henceforward his chief but by no means his only interests, for he was a man of prodigious energy, intelligence and influence and altogether a most notable, if somewhat intimidating, addition to the Society's membership.

It was somewhat disconcerting for the writer to discover, after only cursory research, that Riddell concealed a modest birth and upbringing by putting it about that he was born "in Duns, Berwickshire, the son of a civil servant" (I quote from *The Times* obituary) and that he started his career in law as an articled clerk to a solicitor in Darlington, as he told Bernard Darwin. Riddell was the surname of an aristocratic Border family, which may explain his fiction, but the facts – disclosed in the *Dictionary of National Biography* long after his death – were that he was born in May 1865, the son of a Brixton photographer and educated "privately". His first job was an office boy in a Bloomsbury solicitor's office where, however, he soon so impressed his employer that he was given articles. In 1888, he came top in the First Class honours list of the Solicitors Final examination and was immediately made a partner in his benefactor's firm. Unsurprisingly this had become, by 1903, "Riddell & Co" – occupying 9 John Street, Bedford Row.

The excellent history of Walton Heath Golf Club – *Heather and Heaven* (Phil Pilley 2003) – devotes a whole chapter to George Riddell under the title "The Great Dictator" and leaves little doubt that he could be a ruthless man of business.

Late in 1905, Riddell in partnership with two friends – but with the lion's share – bought the Club from its founder and owner, Sir Cosmo Bonsor. From that moment he became, until his death in December 1934, Walton Heath's undisputed ruler.

He was also very much the proprietor, and (in modern terms) chief executive, of the *News of the World* which, under his energetic and ingenious guidance,

The Bishop of London driving in 1914. He devoted a day a week to golf and Riddell made him an honorary member of Walton Heath as part of his endeavours to attract the great and the good

built up its Sunday circulation to a world record seven million copies and in consequence acquired a considerable political influence, though among the masses rather than the elite, who read Lord Northcliffe's *Times*.

At Walton Heath Riddell became close to politicians, chief among them David Lloyd George, another solicitor. In June of the tropical summer of 1911, Riddell was to note in his diary that the Home Secretary, Winston Churchill, usually played with him twice a week. There were also frequent golfing days at Walton Heath for other members of the Cabinet (sometimes accompanied by their wives). On one occasion the Bishop of London, encountered in the Walton Heath clubhouse, enquired, "How's the Cabinet's game?" and, on a visit to Lord Northcliffe, Riddell was complimented for making golf so popular with Fleet Street.

Along with these politicians and journalists, the Society enjoyed Riddell's hospitality on regular visits to Walton Heath until his death in 1934.

George Riddell presented a match-play Challenge Cup to the Society in 1905. In 1907 he was elected to the Committee though, as might be expected, he was only able rarely to attend meetings – in fact only one at Berners Street. His other two attendances were at the Cafe Royal for the annual dinner, where the official business was confined to the election of new members.

In July 1909, he was knighted and the following year was elected Captain of the Society. Again, his attendances at Committee meetings were sparse, but he was always said to be available on the telephone – his preferred way of doing business. He was President of the Society from 1911 to 1913 and again from 1926 until his death in 1934 when the Society's Summer meetings were held at Walton Heath. Dinners were held by the Society in his honour in 1929 and 1932, once again back at the Cafe Royal, with the entertainment paid for by him as in the pre-war days.

In 1918 he was elevated to a baronetcy and in 1920 created Lord Riddell of Walton Heath. He was a considerable philanthropist – the Royal Free Hospital, where he was President, being among his beneficiaries. After he became President for the second time, the Society began paying an annual sum to the Royal Free and, following his death, the Society paid a sum of £150, of which £136 was raised from the membership.

He did much to encourage artisan golf by founding, with JH Taylor, the Artisans' Golfing Association, and professional golf by the institution of the *News*

of the World match-play championship, one of the most interesting and successful events in the history of the game – though sadly not suited to the economics of professional golf today.

Bernard Darwin owed his job as golf correspondent to *Country Life* to a recommendation from George Riddell to its founder, Edward Hudson – one of the co-owners of the Walton Heath Club. Darwin soon thereafter found himself Hon. Secretary of the London Press Golfing Society, against whom LSGS played an annual match – from 1906 always at Walton Heath.

Riddell buying off photographers who were interrupting a match at Walton Heath in 1914. He is writing instructions to the steward for the photographers to be given a free champagne lunch and then despatched to the station

To Darwin, Lord Riddell was "a good and faithful friend … a man of remarkable force of character … an admirable man of business with much kindness in him and, I suppose, a touch of ruthlessness where it was necessary". And "my own feeling is that though he was successful in the newspaper world, he was really first and foremost a lawyer" – a statement Darwin was qualified to make having been, albeit briefly, both a solicitor and a barrister. As a golfer, Darwin said of Riddell, "he had, and this a high compliment, the qualities of a foursomes player, great resolution and a willingness, entirely devoid of vanity, to subordinate his game to that of a dominant partner for the good of the side".

Darwin wrote from personal knowledge as he was frequently invited to play with Riddell at Walton Heath – and had to buy a padded overcoat in order to

James Beale as the Victorian man of affairs. This portrait still hangs in his great house, Standen

survive winter journeys there in Riddell's open Daimler. It can also be noted that they were both members of the Golf Match Club – dining and match-making, where they would meet, as fellow-members, Charles Murray Smith, Herbert Taylor and Vi Pollock.

Lord Riddell died, without heir, on 5th December 1934: the list of those attending his funeral occupied half-a-page in *The Times*: LSGS was well represented. His interest in the Walton Heath Golf Club was thereafter acquired by the *News of the World*.

Of the other "prominent" members in the Society's early years the writer can only make a few random remarks.

Two Presidents of the Law Society, Thomas Rawle and James Samuel Beale, were both also Presidents of LSGS – the latter for four years in all. He, Beale, was noted for com-

missioning the great Victorian architect Philip Webb in 1892 to build him a remarkable house, near East Grinstead, called Standen. Helen, his unmarried daughter, continued to live there, maintaining it meticulously, until her death in 1972, when she bequeathed it to the National Trust. As one might expect, Beale joined Royal Ashdown Forest GC – scene of many Society meeting and matches – to whom he presented the Standen Cup, which was first won by Horace Hutchinson.

James Beale and his brother, partner in the Birmingham office of Beale & Co, were the joint legal advisers to the Midland Railway. It is worthy of note that LSGS members were also in charge of the legal affairs of three other main-line railways – Cyril Plummer (LSGS Captain in 1907) at Paddington, Edward Moore at Liverpool Street and, as we shall see, ROJ Dallmeyer at Marylebone and, later, York.

Henry Mossop, Captain in 1912 and previously an assiduous Committee member, lived at Ashford and was senior partner of Henry Mossop & Syms, Lincoln's Inn Field. Mossop was one of three cousins, from an old Cumbrian family, who were early pillars of Ashford Manor GC, and he acted on the purchase of the course and later followed Harold Hilton as Ashford's captain. Henry Mossop played a lot of golf at Aldeburgh and was a consistent prize-winner there both in medal and match-play, often in close contention with Aldeburgh's young star, Victor Longstaffe.

Two early members of the Society provide interesting links to the match against the Writers to the Signet GC, instituted in 1961.

Richard Dallmeyer moved from Marylebone, the last terminus to be built for a main line, to York in 1907 but he continued to support the Society and play in

"The Spalding Special," made of five of the latest Pullman Palace Dining Cars, in which will take golfers down to Sandwich for the Amateur Championship.

ATEUR CHAMPIONSHIP,

SANDWICH.

Y 19, 20, 21, & 22, 1914.

A. G. SPALDING & BROS.

easure in announcing that they have made arrangements

to run

PECIAL EXPRESS TRAIN

each day, composed exclusively of

LLMAN PALACE DINING CARS

for the convenience of golfers.

Interior of one of the Pullman Palace Cars on the "Spalding Special," in which breakfast and dinner will be served to golfers en route to the Amateur Championship.

Departure. — The train will leave Charing Cross on each morning at 7.45 a.m. (London Bridge 7.50) and arrive at Sandwich at 9.45 a.m. Table d'hote breakfast will be served immediately after leaving London.

Returning. — The express will depart from Sandwich at 6.35 p.m., and arrive in London about 8.35. Table d'hote dinner will be served immediately after leaving Sandwich.

Fare. — An inclusive charge of 25s. will be made each day for the round trip, to include Reserved Seat in a Pullman Dining Car, Breakfast and Dinner.

Tickets. — As the accommodation will be strictly limited to 110 reserved seats, early application should be made to A. G. Spalding & Bros.,

　　317 & 318, High Holborn, W.C. (Telephone, 230 City) ;
　　29, Haymarket, S.W. (Telephone, 241 City) ; or
　　78, Cheapside, E.C. (Telephone, 446 City),

where plans of the train may be seen and seats booked.

　　No tickets for these Special Trains will be on sale by the Railway Co., and no tickets will be sold on the day of departure.

A. G. SPALDING & BROS.,

317 and 318 HIGH HOLBORN, LONDON, W.C. ;

78 Cheapside, London, E.C.; 　 29 Haymarket, London, S.W. ; 　 New Street House, Birmingham ; 　 4 Oxford Street and 1 Lower Moseley Street, Manchester ; 　 72 Lord Street, Liverpool ; 　 3 South Charlotte Street (Princes St.), Edinburgh ; 　 68 Buchanan Street, Glasgow ; 　 35 Boulevard des Capucines, Paris.

---

matches when his golfing quality was needed (he was a finalist in the Irish Amateur Championship in 1898, losing at the 37th hole). He became Solicitor to the London and North Eastern Railway after its formation in 1924 and in 1934 he was Captain of the London Solicitors' Golfing Society when his son, CJY (Jimmy) Dallmeyer won the scratch prize at Walton Heath in the Society's Summer meeting. As will be told, the record of this success in the Society's records led to the challenge to the Writers to the Signet Golf Club in 1961.

David Kenneth Watson, elected a member in 1904, was the son of William Watson, Lord Advocate of Scotland who became a Law Lord under the title Lord Watson of Thankerton. He gave his address as "c/o Collyer-Bristow & Co, Bedford Row" but in fact he was practising in the firm of Webster & Watson in Newton Abbot, Devon – so he qualified for membership as perhaps the first person "formerly practising in the Metropolitan area", although the qualification was only formally introduced a little later. That he was an excellent golfer is demonstrated by his victory by 5 and 4 over Bruce Kerr in the match against the Bar Golfing Society in 1906.

Trains were important in 1914 and Spalding commissioned a special train for the Amateur Championship at Royal St George's

---

Sunningdale during the London Amateur Foursomes in 1911. The 5th and 6th holes remain little changed but this view is now much restricted by the growth of trees. Some of the bumps have been taken out of the 4th green, a hole Harold Hilton disliked, but its slopes remain tricky

The previous year the Committee "agreed that the Hon. D K Watson be asked to raise a team against the Actors' Golfing Society" who were "anxious to arrange a match". This was not the Stage Golfing Society but, it seems, the George Edwardes Golfing Society, named after the popular manager of Daly's Theatre, whose inaugural golf meeting, attended by Gerald du Maurier, had been reported in *Golf Illustrated* four days previously. One could speculate why the youthful Mr Watson from Newton Abbot was the Committee's choice – could he have been a devotee of the musical comedies staged at Daly's?

How pleasant it would have been for Leslie Nathanson, Captain of the Society against the Writers to the Signet GC in 1961, to have been able to tell his war-time friend and fellow officer, Douglas Watson, the son of one of "DK"'s older brothers, that his uncle had been one of the earliest members of LSGS.

Frank Stone was elected in 1914, the only new member to be elected after the outbreak of war. This was almost certainly because his Blackheath rugby team mate, Robert Pillman, had encouraged him to join. He and Pillman had played for England against France at rugby earlier that year and Stone, having survived the war, returning with the rank of Lt Colonel and a MC, became a partner in the City firm of Stones, Morris and Stone. He was a member of the Sidcup Golf Club which, in the twenties, could field a strong team, including Harold Gillies whose famous plastic surgery unit was based at Sidcup Hospital.

Frank Stone's name can be linked with two other LSGS members already mentioned for their achievements in the early annals of the Halford Hewitt, instituted in 1924 and since 1925 played at Deal where our story began.

So, by way of happy ending, we can conclude with a note of the occasions on which these three LSGS members reached the final of the Hewitt between 1924 and 1932:

1924 V A Pollock (Eton) – winners
1925 V A Pollock (Eton) – winners
1925 F Le S Stone (Harrow) – runners-up
1927 F Le S Stone (Harrow) – winners
1928 V C H Longstaffe (Charterhouse) – runners-up
1929 F Le S Stone (Harrow) – winners
1929 V C H Longstaffe (Charterhouse) – runners-up
1930 V C H Longstaffe (Charterhouse) – winners
1931 F Le S Stone (Harrow) – winners
1932 V C H Longstaffe (Charterhouse) – winners

An advertisement for Kite and Buzzard balls in 1908 – two of the new rubber-cored balls

CHAPTER THREE

Lloyd George and George Riddell

Lloyd George in the water at Littlestone in 1911: a champion of golf but not a champion golfer

DAVID LLOYD GEORGE and George Riddell were by far the most powerful men to have been President of the London Solicitors' Golfing Society and they were closely connected.

The two men were born within two years of each other, in each case into relatively humble families. Both had lost their fathers at a very young age and Lloyd George, like Riddell, began his career at the age of 16 as a clerk in a solicitors' office, before impressing sufficiently to be given articles to qualify as a solicitor. In 1885 Lloyd George set up his own practice in Criccieth in North Wales, and two years later was joined as a partner by his brother William. It was this practice which funded Lloyd George's political career after 1890 when he became the MP for Carnavon (the anglicised name was the official one) as MPs were then unpaid. William continued to work in the practice until shortly before his death in 1967 at the age of 101: almost 80 years of continuous practice, well over twice the career of even the most tireless modern solicitor. David Lloyd George was always an enthusiastic, if not highly skilled, golfer: "a champion of golf but not a champion golfer". But this has not prevented virtually every golf course in North Wales claiming some connection with him. A little later, *World of Golf* commented that he played a round at Deal against bogey. "He received a stroke a hole; he finished 17 down after 18 holes, and he returned his card. To hand in such a record of tragedy a man must be made of stern material."

It is believed that Lloyd George met Riddell, who had by then left the law for newspapers, following Riddell's purchase, with others, of the *Western Mail*. Riddell cultivated the connection as Lloyd George began his rise in the political world and, as the effective proprietor of Walton Heath, in 1907 he persuaded Lloyd George to become a member. This was during the relatively short period when golf, and Walton Heath in particular, became fashionable among the rich and well connected, particularly politicians. Three other Prime Ministers have also been members of the club; Balfour, Bonar Law and Churchill. Riddell was assiduous in cultivating these connections and Horace Hutchinson thought that

much of the early success of Walton Heath was due to his energy and drive. Lloyd George, like Riddell, was not just playing golf. He noted, "You get to know more of a man in a round of golf than in six months of political experience".

Riddell and Lloyd George became close and Riddell's three volumes of diaries record almost 700 meetings with Lloyd George, mostly at Walton Heath over golf. As the Walton Heath history records, Riddell became Lloyd George's "audience, listening post, informant, occasional adviser and general confidant". He also provided favours: including the use of his Rolls Royce and London house, honorary membership at the club and, most generously, the building for Lloyd George of a house close to the clubhouse, Cliftondown, for £2,000.

Today it seems astonishing that a house could be provided near the course at Walton Heath for a leading politician. There was no secret about it: the bombing of the house by suffragettes in the course of its construction was "a sensation the world over" when it happened one night in February 1913. Mrs Pankhurst had been making inflammatory speeches advocating acts of vandalism, particularly against golf clubs. Lloyd George apologised to Riddell for being "such a

Lloyd George seems to be playing in the wrong direction on the 16th (then the 17th) at Walton Heath, watched by, from left, James Braid, Herbert Fowler, the course architect, and Riddell

(left) Lloyd George and Riddell outside Cliftondown

(right) Mr Justice Lush at Lytham in 1911. Two years later he was the judge at Mrs Pankhurst's trial

troublesome and expensive tenant" and wanted her sued for damages: the judicious Riddell noted in his diary that he would do nothing of the sort. Nothing, however, would get in the way of criminal justice. The presiding judge at the Old Bailey for Mrs Pankhurst's trial for inciting the bombing was Mr Justice Lush, who was himself a keen golfer and had been captain of the Bar Golfing Society two years before. He was also the author of the book *The Law of Husband and Wife*, which was probably not to be found on Mrs Pankhurst's bedside table. The jury, effectively at the direction of the judge, found her guilty of the incitement charge but put in a strong plea for mercy: Mr Justice Lush sentenced her to three years penal servitude. There was an immediate outcry and he had to clear the court of women singing the *Women's Marseillaise*. Later that summer there was a heavy police presence at Rye for the Bar Tournament in case of further attacks by suffragettes. To complete the golfing connection, the Home Secretary at the time was Reginald McKenna, also a member of Walton Heath, who had himself been set upon the previous year by two suffragettes at Dornoch. Eight years later, Mr Justice Lush, along with Lloyd George and Riddell, was one of the seven guests of honour invited to the Society's dinner in 1921.

It is believed by some that the actual perpetrator of the bombing was Emily Davidson, who threw herself in front of the King's horse at the Derby a few months later.

After it was rebuilt, Cliftondown was also often used by Frances Stevenson,

Lloyd George's secretary and, from 1913, his mistress. Riddell was aware of the relationship and was largely responsible for making sure that it kept out of the press. Frances Stevenson was nervous about Riddell (as were many others) and commented on that austere man and his penetrating eyes. But there is a suggestion that Riddell was also an admirer of hers, and he left her £1,000 in his will, the same amount he left to Lloyd George and Churchill.

Although the London Solicitors' GS had patriotically suspended its activities during the war, the politicians, as usual, thought such constraints should not apply to them and continued to enjoy regular golf. Walton Heath was full of red Cabinet boxes, policemen and political gossip. Lloyd George had to reprimand Winston Churchill for disclosing to Riddell that Churchill was about to be involved in an imminent Cabinet reshuffle. Lloyd George could occasionally hear the gunfire from the Front when the wind was in the East, and in 1917 he heard the detonation of the mines under the Messines ridge when he was on the 8th hole. These days, unfortunately, he would only hear the rolling barrage of the heavy traffic on the M25. This golfing activity by politicians was surprisingly well known and the regularity of Lloyd George's golf formed the basis of an unlikely plot: in 1917 three communist sympathisers were convicted of treason for conspiring to murder Lloyd George with a poison dart on the golf course.

As the war went on, and particularly after Lloyd George became prime minister in 1916, Riddell was close to the heart of government and very influential, perhaps because he was perceived as not being a direct threat to the politicians. Extraordinarily, after the War Lloyd George appointed Riddell as the Government's press liaison officer and he attended all the post war peace conferences alongside the Prime Minister. In this poacher turned gamekeeper role, Riddell was probably involved in what we tend to think of as the modern art of off-the-record briefing, counter-briefing and leaking.

The ennoblement of George Riddell in 1920, as a newspaper proprietor and close friend of Lloyd George, was controversial. Although this was at the beginning of the original cash for honours scandal, there is no suggestion that Riddell

(left) Herbert Fowler plays towards the 2nd green at Walton Heath in 1904. The filling in of the ditch has made the hole much easier

(right) The 6th green (now the 5th) at Walton Heath in 1904 was originally played as a short hole. Niblick commented at the time that many a card would be spoilt by it. The green remains one of the most difficult in southern England

made any direct payment: he had after all already provided considerable services and favours to Lloyd George. Indeed two years later in his diaries he complains that the cash requirements for a peerage had become all too transparent. Lloyd George did however have to fight hard to overcome the strong objections of the King to the creation of the first divorced peer.

Although Sir Ellis Cunliffe suggested that Lloyd George might be his successor as President of the Society, it was surely Lord Riddell who, in 1921, secured this unlikely acceptance of office by a serving Prime Minister.

Lloyd George only served one year as President and there is no record of him ever playing in a LSGS match or competition. Perhaps his resignation as President might have been prompted by a somewhat gauche enquiry from the Society's secretary as to whether the President was minded to present a prize at the Society's Autumn Meeting. Riddell, if he had been consulted, would surely have advised that it was foolish to trouble him at all, particularly as the Prime Minister was more used to receiving prizes than giving them.

But it was in January 1922, as the serving President of the London Solicitors' Golfing Society as well as Prime Minister, that Lloyd George, as well as Riddell, was involved in a game of golf which caused an international incident. At that time there were economic difficulties throughout Europe, Maynard Keynes had published his influential work *The Economic Consequences of the Peace*, and in Germany the mark was collapsing and hyper-inflation was starting. Lloyd George and Riddell were at a conference in Cannes to discuss the issue of war reparations, on which radically different views were held by the British and

Lloyd George watching Briand, the Prime Minister of France, struggling at golf at Cannes. Gripping the club with his left hand below the right did not help. To Lloyd George's left are Lord Riddell and Bonomi, the Italian prime minister (with club over his arm)

French governments. As is often the case, the important event happened outside the conference sessions when the major players escaped to lunch at Cannes Golf Club.

After a long and noisy lunch Lloyd George persuaded Briand, the Prime Minister of France, and Bonomi, the Prime Minister of Italy, to join him on the golf course. Riddell was also involved in a rather awkward sixsome, which also included Bonar Law, another Walton Heath member and who would later that year himself become Prime Minister. After two terrible shots from the continental Prime Ministers (who were novices), Riddell hit a fine iron shot near the green. Briand congratulated him by saying: "He launches the ball with the same assurance he launches false news in the press". Lloyd George was also able to hit some good shots.

Briand continued to struggle and came up with a Gallic interpretation of Mark Twain's comment about a good walk spoiled. "It is a game for schoolboys", he complained to Lloyd George. "Englishmen never cease to be children. Cannot you enjoy a country walk without hitting a silly little ball?"

Unfortunately for Briand, photographers were present and news of the French sporting humiliation quickly got into the papers. The French took a dim view of their Prime Minister receiving golf lessons from Lloyd George and thought it showed an inexperienced and naive French leader being hoodwinked by the wily Welshman. Briand was forced to return to Paris within days and was out of office shortly thereafter. Bonomi also did not survive as Prime Minister of Italy for long and by the end of 1922 Mussolini, who was at Cannes as a journalist, had seized power.

We cannot tell whether this incident was in any way premeditated by Lloyd George, but, as a famous teetotaller, he would have been sober after the lunch as well as having superior golfing skills. Riddell, despite being a generous host at the Society's meetings at Walton Heath, was also personally very abstemious with alcohol, although perhaps not the teetotaller he had claimed to be at a disarmament conference the previous month in Prohibition-era New York.

What can be said with certainty is that this was the only time the golfing prowess of the President of the Society has precipitated the collapse of a government.

CHAPTER FOUR

The Society affected by War
1914 to 1948

THE OUTBREAK of the First World War in August 1914 shattered the stability and confidence of the Edwardian era. It also meant the immediate end of the first golden age of the London Solicitors' Golfing Society: an age of rapidly increasing membership and fixtures, an impressive accumulation of silver and the wealth and time for solicitors to compete for them. Just a few weeks earlier, on 4th July 1914, 68 members had participated in the Society's Summer meeting at Ashford Manor Golf Club, close to the previous year's record of 86 participants. There were six competitions at the meeting, each with its own cup or other prize, a record for the Society, including a gold medal for the scratch prize which had been instituted the previous year. Despite the assassination in Sarajevo of Archduke Franz Ferdinand six days earlier, it would not have seemed credible to those taking part that the Society would be fully operational for just half the years between 1914 and 1948: only between 1921 and 1937.

Robert Pillman, the winner of the gold medal at Ashford Manor and a scratch handicap player, could acknowledge the LSGS members' applause and reflect on a splendid year in rugby as well as golf, and on the prospect of qualifying as a solicitor. He had already been part of the London Counties team which had famously beaten South Africa 10-8 at Twickenham in 1912 with two vital con-

The French go over for a try in the rugby international in Paris in 1914 despite the English tackles and a stray dog. 11 of the 30 players in the match were to be killed in the First World War

versions by his fellow Blackheath teammate and future LSGS member Francis Stone. In April 1914 he and Frank Stone won their first caps for England in the 39-13 victory against France at Stade de Colombes.

Pillman must have been quickly on the train and ferry that week in April 1914 as, after surviving some rough play by the French in the international on Monday, he was playing in the first round of the London Amateur Foursomes at Harry Colt's still new St George's Hill on Thursday. Not only that, but he and his partner won their match for Sidcup against Mid-Surrey, one of the favourites. Bernard Darwin was playing a few matches ahead and commented in *The Times*, "Mr R.L.Pillman, the football player, not merely refrained from putting ill, which was a considerable achievement, but actually putted extremely well, which was barely decent". The London Amateur Foursomes was an important competition, with each major London club represented by one pair in the scratch knock-out event. Many of the names in the Society's pre-war days were playing at St George's Hill that day. Herbert Taylor was playing for Coombe Hill, yet another of his many clubs, defending the title he had won the previous year. Victor Longstaffe, for Stoke Poges, lost to Bernard Darwin's Woking. Harold Hilton was playing for Ashford Manor with Henry Mossop's cousin, although they managed to halve the 1st hole in nine, and Gilbert Jessop was also in action. But the largest crowd of the day was many miles away at Westward Ho! where Vivian Pollock was playing a match against Jerome Travers, the US Amateur champion, who was playing ominously well.

All this was to change on the outbreak of war that August. Initially, there was optimism generally, and in the Society, as to the duration and cost of the War. The Captain of the Society, Rothwell Haslam, "hardly thought it necessary " to abandon the Autumn meeting, but he was overruled by the Committee and members were asked to contribute five shillings each to the Prisoners of War Relief Fund, "which would have been roughly the cost of attending the meeting". In 1915 there was still some confidence when the Committee resolved that the "Summer meeting be not held if the war continues so long" and the Spring match play competition was held on the basis that these were purely private matches and would not be likely to appear in the papers and attract adverse comment. By 1916, however, all hope had gone, the match play competition was not held and the Committee, after patriotically agreeing to buy £50 of 4 ½ % War Loan, abandoned the Society's activities for the duration of the war.

The huge loss of life and the suffering in the trenches profoundly affected every level of British society. It will never be known how many members, and, of just as much importance, how many prospective members, of the Society lost their lives. One quarter of the Oxford and Cambridge graduates and under-graduates under the age of 25 who served in the British army in 1914 were killed. It was reported in July 1917, that of the nine amateurs who had finished the Open at Prestwick in 1914, two had been killed, two had been wounded and a fifth captured, and some of the nine were past service age. J L C Jenkins, the surprise Amateur Champion in 1914, was wounded during the war and was never quite the same player again.

Sportsmen were particularly encouraged to join up. Field Marshall Lord Roberts said "This is not the time to play games". *The Times* noted in November 1914 that every player who represented England in rugby internationals the previous season had joined the colours. Of the thirty players playing for England and France at Stade de Colombes in 1914, eleven (6 English and 5 French) were killed in the War and in total 27 English rugby internationals lost their lives. For Robert Pillman there were to be no more England caps or gold medal wins and he never qualified as a solicitor. He enlisted as a private on 1st September 1914: by 1916 he was a Captain in the Queen's Own Royal West Kent Regiment. In the trenches he volunteered for bombing raids and once carried a gassed man on his back to safety through 300 yards of no-man's land. He was killed in July 1916 during the Somme offensive, leading a night raid on German lines. He was just 23.

At the end of the war the London Solicitors' GS had to deal with the sudden reversal of the rapid growth of the membership in the early years, up to 209 members after just the first year increasing to 316 reported at the 1910 annual general meeting. By June 1919, the membership had fallen to 249, of whom 23 were life members, and this was almost certainly an overestimate. There were only 126 new members between 1916 and 1926 and at least as many resignations and deaths. The Committee could probably have done better, but the core reason for the lack of recovery in numbers is a simple and tragic fact: not enough young men.

Weeding at Woking in 1910. After the First World War many clubs found it difficult to continue with such labour intensive practices

It was no wonder that it took some time for the Society to resume its activities. A Peace Dinner was planned for 1919 but eventually was held in February 1920. Although it had been hoped that Lloyd George could be persuaded to attend "through the united efforts of Sir Ellis Cunliffe and Sir George Riddell" it is presumed that he was too busy to be there. But the following year the Society achieved the distinction of having the Prime Minister as President as described in the previous chapter.

The golf took even longer to get back to its pre-war levels of activities in what were economically difficult times. There was a final Summer meeting at Ashford Manor in 1919 but not much external activity in that year or the next. The competitors in the Summer meeting

Golfing
and Ladies' Golf.
———
FEBRUARY, 1922.

(top) Golf balls were expensive and it was worth making an effort to find them

(bottom) Winter golf for the well off in 1922 was in the south of France. Lloyd George was a regular visitor and had a hole in one at Nice in 1908. Here the Society's President watches a putt on the 9th green at Cannes

must have been out of practice as Robson Sadler (who was to be Captain in 1924 and later presented the Richardson Sadler Challenge Cup) and T K Langdale tied for the Captain's Prize with a net 88 (gross 100 and 102 respectively). To take account of the perceived lack of activity, the Committee agreed that all those who had paid their subscriptions for 1920 should have them carried over to 1921.

In January 1921 the Sporting Editor of *The Times* had suggested that the Society should provide a representative on a committee of four on the question of the increase of the cost of golf since the war. Golf courses generally were finding it hard to make ends meet and it was becoming more difficult for the Society to find courses where members could play in matches and meetings without the payment of green fees. Following the death of Henry Mossop, Ashford Manor Golf Club was no longer prepared to allow the Society to play its Summer meetings free of charge on a Saturday and these were moved to mid week on different courses. The modern members of the Society would not readily recognise some of the courses used; much depended on the contacts of individual members and their ability to obtain "the courtesy of the course".

1921, however, saw the rebirth of the regular matches and meetings. In January 1921, in the inaugural playing of the Ellis Cunliffe Challenge Vase, Sydney Newman (5) beat L Webster (1) in the final at the Addington. Sydney Newman was a popular figure and served two terms as Captain in 1928 and 1929 and also had the distinction of winning at least two scratch medals at Society meetings. He was later made an honorary life member.

By 1922 the list of matches included the Bar, the Stage, the Auctioneers, Ladies' Legal, the House of Commons, the Engineers and Bramshot GC (which did not survive the Second War but was remembered many years later by Bryan (Peter) Tassell as a "good gorse and heather course"). Some of the other matches took longer to get going and some new ones were started which have not survived, such as matches against the Bishop and Clergy of St Albans, the Junior Constitutional Club and the Paper Trade. Over this period, despite a shortage of numbers, the Society was winning more matches than it was losing, although there was less intensity in the matches than in the days before the war.

As a reminder of those days, in May 1923, the two golfing giants of the early Society, Herbert Taylor and Vivian Pollock, played together in the R&A Spring Medal. Despite a 6 at the 10th and finishing with a 6 and a 5, Vivian Pollock holed the Old Course in 79 which won the Silver Cross of St Andrews for the best scratch score, after an 18 hole play-off. This set him up also to win the George Glennie Medal for the best combined scratch score at the Spring and Autumn meetings in that year. Perhaps the wind was from the right on the way home. Bernard Darwin knew "Mr V A Pollock's joy in the "Guardbridge" wind at St Andrews. He always lashed the ball with a fine dash, but when he was on his homeward way with that wind coming a little from the right, he fairly flung himself at the ball in an ecstasy of confidence".

Vivian Pollock driving in September 1922

The next year Herbert Taylor repeated the feat of winning the combined scratch medal. Cyril Tolley prevented the hat trick in 1925 but Taylor won again in 1928, making three victories by LSGS members in 6 years. Seemingly improving with the years, in 1933 at the age of 64, Taylor won the R&A Autumn scratch medal with a 73 which was just one shot more than the best score ever previously recorded in a R&A medal.

On 25th September 1928, just a few days after his second combined scratch medal, the austere looking Herbert Taylor revealed himself as something of a showman in playing a midnight foursomes match against Vivian Pollock over the 1st and 18th on the Old Course. The illuminations were supplied by car headlights, Chinese lanterns held by the fore-caddies, torches and many rockets. Five hundred people watched, several ending up in the Swilcan Burn, as Taylor and his partner had a good four at the 1st. The *St Andrews Citizen* said "the illumination of the home green was very effective. There was a mass of coloured electric bulbs, and a Chinese lantern was suspended from the flagstick to indicate the position of the hole. Andrew Kirkcaldy in his official capacity, as professional of the Club, stood beside the hole … The hole was played out, but whether or not the competitors finished with the balls they drove off from the tee is uncertain. At any rate a halved hole was declared." The match was refereed by Provost Boase, a future Captain of the R&A, and sounds semi-official but it is easy to imagine a very po-faced reaction from the present day Links Trust.

Victor Longstaffe, another very good pre-war player for LSGS, was now devoting much of his energy to the Moles GS, which he had co-founded in 1911. Most Society members have stopped in the hall of Woking Golf Club to wonder at the photograph of Bobby Jones in deep rough and to admire the record underneath of the Moles beating the United States in 1926, with Bobby Jones, Francis

From left, John Beck, Francis Ouimet, Tony Torrance and Jesse Guilford at Woking in 1926 for Victor Longstaffe's Moles team against the United States. Beck had a busy day beating Ouimet and halving with Bobby Jones and was, in 1938, the first successful home Walker Cup captain. Among his more obscure achievements was a win against LSGS as a guest for the Writers to the Signet GC in 1969

Ouimet and Jess Sweetser all in the US team. Victor Longstaffe was the non-playing Captain of the Moles that day: it is said that his hospitality at the dinner at the Savoy the previous night was probably the decisive factor. The Americans, however, had revenge later that summer, scraping home 6 ½ to 5 ½ in the Walker Cup at Muirfield, although Bobby Jones beat Cyril Tolley in the singles 12 and 11, a massive margin over their 36 hole match. Bobby Jones also won the Open Championship but Jess Sweetser won the Amateur.

Among the golfing mortals of the Society the knockout handicap match-play contests were particularly popular, and between the wars no fewer than three were played each year: the Spring knock-out (for which the Sir Joseph Hood Challenge Cup had by then been presented), the Riddell Challenge Cup (which was a knock-out after initial qualification) and the Ellis Cunliffe Challenge Vase. These knock-out events fell out of fashion in the 1950s and the magnificent trophies were re-assigned to other events at one of the meetings. By the early 21st century, the Riddell Challenge Cup, the Society's senior trophy, had been relegated to a competition for the over 50s at the Spring meeting, which would not have pleased the great man.

Although a matchplay event was restarted in 2004, it is unlikely that Society members could now manage more than one a year in an age where clients and families take precedence over golf.

In 1925, F Evelyn Jones, not the strongest of players off 16 handicap, won a prize presented by FAS Stern at the Autumn meeting at the Addington with a net 74. He was so delighted that a little later he presented the handsome pair of trophies which are now played for in the afternoon foursomes of the Spring meeting. His son also became a member and won the scratch gold medal in 1930 but was later struck off, because of his "deplorable conduct in a certain financial transaction".

It was a shame that, in 1919, a breakdown in health and pressure of work (his partner Ernest Longstaffe, a former Captain, died the same year) meant that Thomas Fenwick, had to resign as Secretary and Treasurer of the Society. He had been Secretary and Treasurer from the beginning and probably the most important pillar of the Society in its early years, and his meticulous nature was to be sorely missed. His successor, Bertie Trayton Kenward, was a Society regular and a reasonable golfer, having his handicap cut to 4 on winning the Riddell Challenge Cup in 1920, which he won again in 1922 and 1924. He was fond of long handwritten minutes and somewhat archaic language but he seems to have been lacking in both organisation and energy: not good attributes for a secretary. There were early warning signs: the Peace Dinner made a loss probably because of poor budgeting; it took almost a year to pay the toastmaster after a dinner and sub-committees were appointed to help run the Meetings. In 1922 Trayton Kenward was not reappointed as Treasurer but continued as Secretary with Rothwell Haslam and John Woodhouse acting as auditors.

The Riddell Challenge Cup. George Riddell knew how to impress and in 1905 was the first to present the Society with a permanent cup

This was unfortunate as Rothwell Haslam had already fallen out with Kenward in 1921 when he objected to the Secretary consulting Thomas Fenwick over rule changes drafted by Haslam. This sounds uncontroversial, indeed sensible, but Haslam considered it "improper and ultra vires". Rothwell Haslam had been captain of the Society during the war years and had for many years presented a prize for golfers between 11 and 18 handicap, although his handicap, perhaps surprisingly, was a bit better: he had his handicap reduced from 7 to 6 on winning the Riddell Challenge Cup in 1919, the year before Trayton Kenward's first victory. But he was in constant attendance at Committee meetings where he always made comments; in other words he appears to have been an example of the committee busybody.

The final explosion came on 5th April 1922 as very carefully recorded in the minutes by Trayton Kenward, the Secretary, in his best hand. Rothwell Haslam accused Kenward of inserting into the Rules, without the authority of a general meeting or the knowledge of the Committee, a proviso to the effect that the Committee "shall include the nominee of the Law Society's Council". Various letters were produced between the two men. Eventually, the chairman and that year's Captain, Harold Forbes White, ruled that Mr Haslam's accusation was most improper and had no substance and he was asked to apologise. On refusing to do so, he was asked to resign whereupon he left the meeting and later resigned completely from the Society.

The page in the minute book covering the resignation of Rothwell Haslam. Harold Forbes White, the Captain, has added in his own hand, "and asked him to withdraw the allegations and apologise: and on his refusal to do so –"

Secretary had, without the sanction of a General Meeting, and without the knowledge of the Committee, inserted in the 1920 Rules the following words:

"which shall include the nominee of the Law Society's Council."

After reading the correspondence and reference to the various relevant Minutes and in particular, a Minute of a proposal by Mr. Haslam at the Annual General Meeting of the Society on the 25th March 1920, the Chairman ruled that Mr Haslam's letter was most improper and that there was no substance whatsoever in his allegations. *and asked him to withdraw his allegations & apologise; and on his refusal to do so –*: Mr Lionel Webster moved that Mr Haslam should either apologise in writing to the Hon. Secretary and withdraw his allegations, or be asked to resign from the Committee.

Mr James Hall seconded this Motion.

The Chairman asked Mr Haslam

In a coda to this rare moment of discord in the Society's affairs, Haslam and Woodhouse refused, or were unable, to carry out their audit duties and John Woodhouse made a nuisance of himself at the 1923 annual meeting and was eventually asked to leave.

Looking back from the 21st century, a dispute over whether a nominee of the Law Society should be on the Society's Committee seems scarcely credible, but in the 1920s the Law Society was more central to solicitors' practices. Two of the very early Presidents of the Society, Thomas Rawle and James Beale had also become Presidents of the Law Society. The inaugural meeting of the Society had been at the Law Society's Hall and the annual meetings thereafter were always held there, albeit usually mainly attended by committee members. The more sensible arrangement of having them at the end of play at the Spring or Summer Meeting only started in 1949. After the First World War, committee meetings were usually also held at the Law Society's Hall, often in the Council Room, and this continued until the end of the 1960s.

The Society's dinners moved, after the First World War, from the surely more agreeable surroundings of the Cafe Royal to the Law Society's Hall. This must have been done for financial reasons although there were murmurings about the quality of the 21/- menu at the Peace Dinner and the gratuities expected by the Law Society's staff, which had contributed to the overall loss. These murmurings about the Law Society's caterers rumbled on in subsequent years. Nevertheless the Society thought keeping close to the Law Society was important, hence the discussion about its nominee on the Committee which caused the great dispute in 1922. ER Cook, the Secretary General of the Law Society, was President of the Society for 1925-26 and, as Sir Edmund Cook, became a vice president in 1939. Sir Harry Pritchard and Sir Reginald Poole, both Presidents of the Law Society, each became President of the Society after the death of Lord Riddell. Sir Reginald Poole, of Lewis & Lewis, had a long standing connection with the Society having, more than 30 years before, played in the 1904 solicitors' game against the Bar at Deal and attended the meeting forming the Society. He was also the guest of honour at the inaugural dinner of the Association of Women Solicitors. When there was not a specific officeholder, the President of the Law Society was formally elected a vice president at each year's annual meeting of LSGS until 1963 (although it is not clear whether they all knew they were the holder of this office).

Reginald Poole in 1911. He played in the first game against the Bar and was President in the 1930s

The existence of the London Solicitors' GS, in the form of its silverware, was however evident in the Law Society's Hall for all to see and admire. In 1929 the Committee agreed to purchase a cabinet to display all the cups in the Reading Room (directly opposite the main entrance). Eventually in 1931 this ended up in the Library at a cost to LSGS of £25 10 shillings, a substantial sum for those hard pressed times. Unfortunately the display cabinet only saw a few years of use as the trophies were moved in 1940 for safekeeping to the strong room of White & Leonard & Nicholls & Co at 4 St Bride, EC4. In 1946 the cups were cleaned and returned to the show case and the Law Society was asked if this could be moved from the Library to the Common Room. By 1950 the display cabinet was no longer needed as the cups were held by the winners and it was decided to sell it: unfortunately only £7 10 shillings was offered ("on the low side") and the Law

Society was asked to buy it. Whether or not it did so, there is now no evidence of the display cabinet in the rather corporate like surroundings of the modern Law Society's Hall. The most tangible remaining link to the Society is a substantial portrait of the ubiquitous Lord Riddell in the Reading Room.

After the resignation in 1922 of his tormentor, Rothwell Haslam, Trayton Kenward continued as Secretary until 1927 and was even reappointed as Treasurer in 1924. These were difficult times for the Society; the root cause being a shortage of active members. This was compounded by a decision in 1912 to allow members to buy life membership: even though the yearly subscription had been raised in 1920 from 5 shillings to 10, there was insufficient income from subscriptions to meet normal expenditure. After a poor 1926, with only 9 new members, the membership was 250; but, of these, 115 were life members and 25 of the subscription paying members were a year behind. The dinner that year was cancelled for lack of funds and a review was carried out by Committee members of the financial position. Perhaps some of the members were nervously devoting all their attention to the great legislation of 1925, the Law of Property Act, the Settled Land Act, the Land Registration Act and the Trustee Act, which had shaken the stability of the solicitors' world. In 1927 a sensible decision was made to promote Trayton Kenward to Captain and appoint a new Secretary and Treasurer. The person selected was Harold Forbes White, who had been Captain in 1922, and he was to hold both posts for more than 20 years.

Lord Riddell

There was an immediate improvement: the subscription arrears were brought up to date or the laggards expelled, and new members were recruited. The gold medal for the scratch prize at the Summer meeting was reintroduced in 1927, although it died permanently with the Second World War. Things were now left to the Secretary, the number of committee meetings was reduced and the typewriter makes its first appearance in the minute books: the age of the first of the Secretary/Managers had arrived.

This was also the age of Lord Riddell, following his election for a second term as President from 1926 until his death in December 1934. In the pre-war days he had been a fierce competitor. Bernard Darwin said: "He played tolerably well off eight or nine, in a method that looked at first sight wholly prohibitive of success. I have in mind a vivid picture of him putting with his right foot drawn back, while he leered or perhaps I should say

scowled, at the ball over his left shoulder. It looked uncomfortable, but he was a good holer of a putt at a pinch."

Now ill health and arthritis meant that Riddell's playing days were over but he played the role of elder statesman and benefactor to the full. His generosity at Walton Heath certainly helped the Society; after all, the year's subscription of 10 shillings would have been paid for by the day's outing at the Summer meeting, with free golf and lunch and champagne on the 1st tee. Many were the stories passed down to future generations about the hospitality at the Walton Heath days. Adrian Watney remembers a senior partner, Frank Emmet, (who became a member in 1931 probably for this very purpose) telling him it was the only golf he could afford to play at the time. Indeed some members did not even play a second round but continued to enjoy Riddell's generosity through the afternoon.

Unsurprisingly, there was a healthy influx of 195 new members from 1927 (when the Summer meeting moved to Walton Heath) to 1934, with a total membership in January 1935 of 363, exceeding the pre-war number. The Walton Heath Summer meeting was, without doubt, the highlight of the Society's year in the early 1930s. On 12th June 1931 there were 130 entrants, the largest ever, all of whom were somehow fitted on to the Old Course. That morning *The Times* noted "Lord Riddell, the president of the society, will entertain the competitors during the day and at dinner after the meeting".

In 1931 the country was in the depths of the Great Depression and yet at Walton Heath there was entertainment at a level which might have even embarrassed hedge fund managers and investment bankers in the years before the Great Financial Crisis of September 2008. It is not known whether Riddell paid

The medal won by RW Ripley for the best scratch score at the 1933 summer meeting, which many years later was purchased by James Furber

for the hospitality himself or whether it was borne by the Club, even though he never owned more than 83% of the shares. In those days Walton Heath was closely run by Lord Riddell and his wish was all that mattered: if Riddell said hello to somebody at the Club, the steward would not charge for his drinks. These details did not concern the Society's members who enjoyed themselves throughout the day and well into the night. The minutes note that some even assumed that Lord Riddell would pick up the bill for their own caddies: and it is possible that there may have been 130 caddies out that day, representing Walton Heath's full complement.

The scoring at Walton Heath was impressive for the last years of Riddell's life. Rupert Fison, later a good Suffolk golfer, had won the 1931 scratch with a fine 76 and the Society had quickly reduced his handicap to scratch. R W Ripley won with an 80 in 1932 and a 78 in the following year. But Jimmy Dallmeyer capped them all with an excellent 75 in 1934, which also won the handicap event with a 72 off his 3 handicap: perhaps the best score in a meeting to date and in a year when his father, Richard Dallmeyer, was Captain.

Not all the contestants that day in May 1934 were paying proper attention to the golf. Peter Tassell had just joined the Society and seventy years later in 2004, the centenary year, was providing lucid assistance to research into the early members as well as providing a living link with the Riddell days. His only expense at Walton Heath was the competition fee and sweepstake. He was first out at 8.45 am and was back at around 11am. He reports: "We had drinks and an early and leisurely lunch, but it was quite impossible to play a second round as our professional brethren were, one and all, totally tight, and the late starters, availing themselves of free champagne before starting out, seemed … to get into the pond on the first hole, and when they dropped behind and essayed the second time, went straight back into the water. It was a memorable day."

After Riddell's death in December 1934 a final Summer meeting was held at Walton Heath in 1935, when the scratch medal was won by Robert Thairlwall, Peter Tassell's playing partner the previous year, with another good 76 and the club agreed it should be free of green fees, "provided there was no change of ownership". Later that year Lady Riddell sold Riddell's interest in the club and in 1936 the LSGS's Summer meeting moved elsewhere.

Perhaps the last word on Riddell should be left to Bill Deedes, the former editor of the *Telegraph* and the Dear Bill of *Private Eye* renown, and one of the last to have known Riddell personally. Shortly before his death he was asked to guess which of the then contemporary press barons most resembled Lord Copper, the proprietor of the *Daily Beast*, in Evelyn Waugh's brilliant satire *Scoop*. Deedes quickly dismissed Lord Riddell on the basis he was quite simply too competent to qualify.

In the 1930s the Society's golf was being played on other good courses as well as Walton Heath and the move to foursomes golf, the Society's modern preferred method of play, was the subject of a formal decision by the Committee in 1937 when foursomes replaced any fourballs in the Society's matches and meetings. The Society was also continuing rigorously to monitor handicaps, which was usual for societies in the days before standard scratch scoring: a special handicap book was kept for the purpose. A good active member such as Frank Stone (who had survived the War and reached +3) would regularly have his handicap altered and the winner of a major prize could expect a cut in handicap, sometimes of several shots. A new member would be carefully reviewed for handicap: on joining in 1938 Leslie Nathanson was allotted a provisional handicap of 12 but was asked to put in cards on "well known courses" so that his handicap could be considered further. The Society handicap has continued to be applied from time to time: even at the beginning of the 21st century Christopher Johnson-Gilbert had a special, much lower, Society handicap during the time it took for his actual club handicap to catch up with his considerable golfing ability. In 1931 the Committee came up with an adjustment for home advantage when it ruled that in knock-out competitions "a member who plays on his own course shall allow one stroke to his opponent, after all allowance for handicaps".

Sir Ellis Cunliffe: Solicitor to the Board of Trade and organiser of the Titanic inquiry

The 1920s and 30s, the era of Fred Astaire, was also an age of formal wear: the dinner jacket was the height of fashion. There were regular Society dinners and in the early days some had musical entertainments afterwards, often funded by Riddell. There was even a suggestion in 1931 for a dance, but this idea was quickly abandoned. Ever since 1911 there had been suggestions that ladies might be invited to dinners but this appears not to have happened.

The Presidents of the Society in the period from 1914 to 1948 merit a special mention. Reference has already been made to the Law Society connection, but the other Presidents show the extent to which solicitors were then involved in politics and government. Lloyd George and Lord Riddell, of course, are sufficiently important to have their own chapter.

Current Society members will know of Ellis Cunliffe only through the handsome vase which is now a prize at the Autumn meeting. In fact Sir Ellis Cunliffe,

Bonar Law and Lloyd George in the spring of 1921 when there was still sweetness between the leaders of the last Conservative/Liberal coalition before 2010

who was President of the Society from 1914 to 1921, was an important figure and for a time in 1912 was very much in the public eye. As Solicitor to the Board of Trade from 1900 to 1920, Sir Ellis Cunliffe had, among many other roles, legal responsibility for Britain's merchant shipping fleet, then still the largest in the world. When the Titanic sank in 1912 there was great public concern that the pride of the British liners, supposedly unsinkable, should have been lost on her maiden voyage with the loss of 1,517 lives. Sir Ellis was in charge of organising the wreck inquiry, which attracted great public interest, and he instructed five counsel including the Attorney General and the Solicitor General to represent the Board of Trade. Very early on he had clear views on the actions of the SS California which had been passed by the Titanic shortly before she hit the ice, and these views were shared when the Inquiry found that the California and her captain had failed properly to respond to the Titanic's distress signals.

As Solicitor to the Board of Trade, Ellis Cunliffe would have worked closely with David Lloyd George who was President of the Board of Trade from 1905 to 1908. Like everybody else of substance, he knew George Riddell and probably had dealings with him when, later in his career, he was Chairman of the Kensington, Fulham and Chelsea General Hospital and Riddell was President of the Royal Free Hospital.

There is an interesting political twist to the election in 1922 of Sir Joseph Hood as President of the Society in succession to David Lloyd George. Lloyd George was still Prime Minister of the last Liberal/Conservative ruling coalition before 2010 but Lord Riddell was that year to switch the political support of his newspapers, including *The News of the World*, from the Liberals led by Lloyd George to the Conservatives under Bonar Law. The Conservatives duly won the general election later that year and Bonar Law became Prime Minister. Sir Joseph Hood Bt MP was the Conservative Member of Parliament for Wimbledon, having previously been the local mayor, and was also the deputy chairman of British American Tobacco. There is nothing to suggest Riddell was involved in the selection but it would be interesting to know if Trayton Kenward had consulted him before making the suggestion at the relevant Committee meeting. Riddell and Hood were then working together on raising funds for a public course in Richmond Park and both were present and spoke when it was opened the following year by the Duke of York, later George VI.

This was the time when the Society's political connections were strongest and in 1923 LSGS beat the House of Commons by 9 matches to four in a handicap game. Robert C Nesbitt, who became the next President of the Society in 1924, was also an MP but it is unlikely that his political connections were relevant. He was senior partner of Markby, Stewart & Wadesons, an active member of the Society, had been on the Committee and was also on the Council of the Law Society from 1909 to 1926. In his youth, he had been a keen cyclist: his records included London to Bath and back in 16 hours 10 minutes on

Robert Nesbitt in 1888. In 1891 he cycled from London to Bath and back in 16 hours 10 minutes

1st August 1891, and 155.5 miles on the North Road in 12 hours on 2nd August 1890. For these achievements, he is forgiven as an MP for taking the whip of the Unionist Party which, in 1922, caused lasting long term damage to Great Britain and Ireland, by helping to procure the separation of Northern Ireland from the newly independent Republic of Ireland.

In 1930, during Lord Riddell's second term as President, another Conservative politician became a vice president. He was Viscount Brentford, better known as William Joynson-Hicks (or "Jix"), who had been Home Secretary from 1924 to 1929. He was responsible for the Equal Franchise Act 1928, finally giving women full voting equality, which gave rise to the completely false rumour, put about by Winston Churchill, that he had done this only because he had promised it to Lady Astor.

Sir Thomas Barnes, who was President from 1938 to 1953, had a career in the civil service, as opposed to politics; but had time for golf off 4 handicap and won the handicap prize at the 1937 Autumn meeting at Sunningdale with a net 71. He was Sir Ellis Cunliffe's successor as Solicitor to the Board of Trade in 1920, appointed at the young age of 32. From there he rose to greater heights when in 1934 he was made Solicitor to the Treasury and King's Proctor, the first solicitor to be appointed to that position. He was highly regarded and was trusted to organise the first major Tribunal of Inquiry, established for the Budget leak of 1936.

The imminence of war in the late 1930s affected the London Solicitors' GS as much as everybody else as attention turned apprehensively to Germany. The signs had been there for some time: even in 1933 the report in *The Times* of the Society's meeting at Walton Heath had appeared under an article on the effects of the Nazis banning certain types of jokes. The Autumn meeting in 1938 was not held because of the "European crisis" and, on the outbreak of the Second World War, the following year, all activities were abandoned.

After the end of the War, although several Committee meetings were held in 1946 there was no golfing activity and even in 1947 there was only a match against the Bar and an Autumn meeting attended by 22 people. These were days of austerity and rationing, with no meat at the 5 shillings lunch at the meeting at Royal Mid Surrey. By now the talk in the minutes was no less than "the question of the rehabilitation of the Society's life". The membership had fallen to a total of 189 in February 1948, 114 ordinary members and 75 life members, just over half the total of 363 members in 1935.

In 1948 things began to change: 27 people attended a lunch at the Law Society's Hall and at the annual meeting afterwards Harold Forbes White, who appeared to have lost the energy he had shown on his appointment almost 21 years before, resigned as Secretary and Treasurer to be replaced by John Haslam of Joynson-Hicks. All the talk, after the formal business, was about the need for younger blood in the Society and it would have been easy for the Society to have quietly faded away. This nearly happened: in July 1948 a letter was sent out to members pointing out the small attendances at meetings and asking whether they were willing to support the Society at the Autumn meeting. The minutes of the Committee ominously record "on the result of the letter to members would depend whether the Committee could justifiably continue to arrange future competitions". In other words, the Society might then have come to an end. Fortunately, energy and initiative were shown the following year by the Committee, helped by the fact that there were more young men available than after the First World War. The re-birth of the Society was imminent.

CHAPTER FIVE

The Birth of the Modern Society
1949 to 1974

IN FEBRUARY 1949 there was a major effort to recruit new members for the London Solicitors' Golfing Society. A circular was printed and sent to all solicitors in London at a cost of £70, a substantial proportion of the remaining funds of the Society. In addition, members of the City of London Solicitors' Company were invited to join. It worked: three months later 39 new members were elected including F R (Bobby) Furber, Robert Stoneham, Francis Perkins and the first female member, Mrs M Satchell, a very good player. At the beginning of 1949 the City firms were substantially under-represented as members of the Society. This was now about to change; by the end of 1950 the future senior partners of Slaughter and May (Peter Marriage), Norton Rose (Giles Botterell) and Herbert Smith (H W (David) Higginson) had all joined. The patronage of the City firms, especially the bringing forward of new members for LSGS, was to prove to be vital. The future of the Society was assured.

Gordon Petch's memory should be toasted at least once a year by the Society, in grateful thanks for what was done in this short period. He proposed the recruitment campaign and produced the draft letter. He had only recently joined the Committee and, quite rightly, was made Captain in 1949, but what was achieved by him and John Haslam, the secretary, was colossal. Apart from the all important new recruits, the practice began of appointing vice captains to ensure continuity, Society ties were introduced, the annual meetings began to be held after one of the golf meetings, the Society's spoons and other trophies were replenished and the matches with other societies were restarted and new matches begun. A booklet was produced and circulated to all members containing

Gordon Petch (right) on the steps of the Royal Ashdown Forest clubhouse in the early 1960s with the Marquis of Aberdeen (centre), the club's president, and Douglas Strain, the secretary

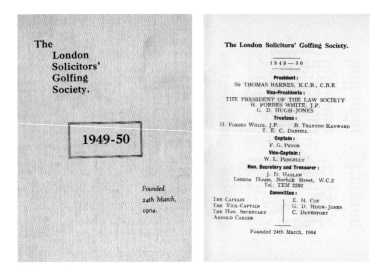

The London
Solicitors'
Golfing
Society.

1949-50

Founded
24th March,
1904.

The London Solicitors' Golfing Society.

1949—50

President :
Sir THOMAS BARNES, K.C.B., C.B.E.
Vice-Presidents :
THE PRESIDENT OF THE LAW SOCIETY
H. FORBES WHITE, J.P.
G. D. HUGH-JONES
Trustees :
H. FORBES WHITE, J.P.   B. TRAYTON KENWARD
T. E. C. DANIELL
Captain :
F. G. PETCH
Vice-Captain :
W. L. PENGELLY
Hon. Secretary and Treasurer :
J. D. HASLAM
Lennox House, Norfolk Street, W.C.2
Tel: TEM 2282
Committee :

THE CAPTAIN	E. H. COE
THE VICE-CAPTAIN	G. D. HUGH-JONES
THE HON. SECRETARY	C. DAVENPORT
ARNOLD CARTER	

Founded 24th March, 1904

details of officers, the Rules, past winners and the names and addresses of all members and the date they became a member. All of this happened in Gordon Petch's year of office in 1949/50. There was now as much energy and enthusiasm as there had been in the very early days and the Society was now aiming for the best courses. The next golden age was about to begin.

Gordon Petch was a good player, reduced to 1 handicap on winning the Ellis Cunliffe Challenge Vase in 1933. In 1948 he won the scratch medal with a 79 at the Summer meeting at Sandy Lodge and also helped to win the first three playings of the Stoneham Porringer, the inter-firm foursomes competition, for Markby, Stewart & Wadesons. Much later he became senior partner of the firm arriving in the office, towards the end of his career, at 10.30am reputedly having already played four holes of golf at Royal Ashdown Forest, where he was captain and president. He also had another excellent attribute for the role of senior partner: he was stone deaf. There is some suggestion that his sense of self importance, vital for the reinvigoration of the London Solicitors'GS, may have led to one or two reinterpretations of his personal history. For example, it was rumoured at Markby's that he had played in the Walker Cup before the war: nobody quite knew how these rumours started, although he did represent the British Seniors in 1954 and 1956 in matches against the seniors from the United States and Canada. He was also President of the Society from 1964 to 1972, perhaps the first to be chosen for his services to the Society rather than his status.

The enthusiasm of the Society now extended to competitive fixtures: the new recruits of Peter Marriage, David Higginson, Bobby Furber and T F P Martin had been immediately deployed against the Bar in 1949 who were beaten 7–1. In 1950 it was decided to try and play fully representative matches, that is to say without handicap, wherever possible, for example against the Bar and the Chartered Accountants. The fresh young players were keen for a challenge. There were still links and concessionary arrangements with Walton Heath and the match there against the Chartered Surveyors was particularly popular in the 1950s. A number of new matches started, for example against the Medical Golfing Society, the Architects and the Wine Trade. The early 1950s also saw a move to have the Society's matches and meetings held on one of the splendid heathland courses south and west of London, with occasional visits north of London, which has continued to the present. The names of Worplesdon, Woking, Walton Heath, the Addington and the Berkshire recur.

The new recruits also turned their attention to the Society's meetings. It is probably fair to say that the standard of golf between the wars had dropped since the triumvirate of Taylor, Pollock and Longstaffe had ceased to be involved in the Society's activities after the First War. Now there were many good young players who began to dominate the meetings.

Harold Meaby had won the "no meat" medal in 1947 with a 78, just weeks after joining, and won scratch prizes again in 1952 and 1958 with the excellent scores of 72 and 75. In later years he and his son Brian formed a competitive pairing for Meaby & Co.

Peter Marriage had an even faster start: he won the 1949 Autumn medal at Wentworth with an 80 and had also played against the Bar before the Committee got round to admitting him as a member in February 1950, at the same time as Jack Watney. Marriage won a scratch prize again in 1951 with a 76 and a final one in 1963, with a 78 at New Zealand.

D I C Cooke had won the scratch medal in the 1949 Summer meeting at West Hill with a 79 and also won the Riddell Cup, still a matchplay competition, that year. At the 1950 Spring meeting at Moor Park, Francis Perkins won the scratch medal with a 76. But it was at the 1950 Autumn meeting at Worplesdon that the new members achieved a clean sweep: Bobby Furber won the scratch with a 78, Jack Watney the handicap and Furber and Marriage the afternoon foursomes. Bobby Furber won scratch medals again in 1955 with a good 74 at Swinley Forest (including coming back in 32) and in 1959, 1961 and 1967.

Many LSGS members play for years with limited success but these young men had all won within 18 months of joining and were to go on to be very important in the post-war success of the Society.

The pleasantly modest fixture card was first distributed in 1954. This was the Society's Golden Jubilee year, when the first dinner after the War was held in the Law Society's Hall. It was thought 52 shillings (£2.60) was the maximum that the members could bear. It was the first dinner to which women were invited and it was a great success. Perhaps the introduction of the silk tie was the culminating step: this finally happened after an admirably persistent cam-

Bobby Furber at the piano entertaining LSGS members in the 1960s

paign by Tom Dinwiddy, another new recruit, who was not going to put up with austerity polyester.

Since the earliest days an honorarium had been paid to the clerk or secretary, always male, who had done most of the administrative work of the London Solicitors' GS in the offices of the Secretary. In 1956 the substantial sum of £31 was raised for Mr Smart who had helped in John Haslam's office. In 1954 some of this burden had been removed when the standing order was introduced for the payment of subscriptions and a separate Treasurer was appointed, although some Treasurers have been more actively involved in actually doing the accounting than others.

In 1953 Sir Thomas Barnes gave up the Presidency of the Society he had held since 1938, at the end of his distinguished career in the civil service. His successor, Sir Dingwall Bateson, was then senior partner of Walters and Hart and President of the Law Society. He had won a MC in the First War and was 7 handicap when he became a member in 1937. Bateson advised Noel Coward on his financial arrangements and had the dubious privilege of being the source of the name of Coward's speedboat, "Dingo". Bateson is reported to have said, somewhat cynically: "a solicitor is a man who calls in a person he doesn't know, to sign a contract he hasn't seen, to buy property he doesn't want, with money he hasn't got".

John Haslam. His years as Secretary, from 1948-1956, were vital for the re-invigoration of LSGS

The Society has, in the main, been blessed with diligent secretaries and John Haslam of Joynson-Hicks, who was also a good cricketer and a charming man, had done a good job in the vital post-war period and was rewarded with the Captaincy in 1956. A little later he was captain and then president of Royal Mid-Surrey, where the Society had played its first meeting in 1904. A room in the new clubhouse is named after him but this does not compensate for the loss of Royal Mid-Surrey's treasures in a fire in 2001, including one of the finest collection of golfing photographs of any club.

His successor as Secretary that year, Bobby Furber, had a few years earlier become a partner in Clifford-Turner, having moved from Slaughter and May following a suggestion made after a Society meeting when he had played with Raymond Clifford-Turner and Francis Perkins. He would in later years become the doyen of the Society, serving continuously on the Committee from 1954 to 1990, a total of 36 years. His term as Secretary saw the continuation and development of the post-war invigoration of the Society. Later as Captain in 1965, Vice President from 1969 to 1982 and President from 1982 to 1990, Bobby Furber has been the central figure of the Society and overseen the continuation of the Society's traditions, particularly foursomes golf.

Furber was Captain of Royal St George's when the Open returned there in 1981 and was later President. He has also been chairman of the Rules Committee of the R&A and is one Britain's few remaining Field Marshalls, holding that position at Royal Blackheath. But, unlike many holders of grand office, he is a man both interesting and interested. He is never more animated than when discussing books or telling anecdotes over a glass of wine; or when playing the piano, as he did so well at Greywalls in the early days of the match against the Writers to the Signet GC.

Bobby Furber also represents a link to the earliest days of the Society. He once scored for Sandy Herd who as long ago as 1892 had been runner-up to Harold Hilton for the Open at its first playing at Muirfield and the first time it had been played over 72 holes. Sandy Herd, notorious as the first club waggler, eventually won the Open himself at Hoylake in 1902, the first year of the rubber-cored Haskell ball. Furber also sat next to Bernard Darwin at a dinner in the Dormy House at Rye in 1949, no doubt learning something of golfing history and, just as importantly, how to convey it lightly. This can be seen from the chapters he has written for this book and, in full, in his excellent history of Royal St George's, *A Course for Heroes*. There are several references to LSGS in the book, including its matches with the Writers to the Signet GC, and the strong-hearted can read more of the sad collapse of the Society's Herbert Taylor in the final of the Amateur in 1908.

Bobby Furber in the uniform of the Field Marshall of Royal Blackheath

In 1950s and 60s the work of London solicitors was primarily UK based and less international than it had been in 1904. Exchange controls were in place, and the acquisition or disposal of even a small foreign business required official approval. The limit of 20 partners in a partnership, which was not abolished until 1968, also had the effect of inhibiting the growth of law firms. Even the largest firms, Linklaters & Paines, Slaughter and May and Freshfields, were tiny by the standards of the 21st century. The globalisation of the provision of legal services and the boom in the size of English law firms was yet to begin. Although post-war rationing had gone on the return of a Conservative government, petrol rationing was re-introduced in 1956 following the Suez debacle causing the Committee to consider the viability of the Society's fixtures: the age of the train to get to golf clubs was now in the past.

It was against this background that the Law Society asked the Society to entertain the American Bar Association which in July 1957 was holding its annual convention in London, for the first time since 1924. An enjoyable 20 a side foursomes match was played at the Berkshire which the Society won 7–3 over the Americans who were entirely unaccustomed to foursomes golf. The ABA presented the Society with a cup which is now awarded for the best scratch score at the Autumn meeting and LSGS presented a putter made by Old Tom Morris to the fortunate ABA Captain, Sidney Wickenhaver. In 1960 the Society

Some very hot participants after the Society's match at Burning Tree in Maryland against the American Bar Association in 1960. Bobby Furber is perching on the left end of the bench next to Edgar Eisenhower, the brother of the American President

Bill Farrer, as captain of the LSGS team, receiving the claret jug at Sunningdale in 1971 for the match against members of the American Bar Association

was involved, with the Bar and Bench, in a return match against the ABA in Washington. Unfortunately the Captain that year, Tom Sowerby, became ill on the boat and Bobby Furber had to assume the captaincy of the Society's team. One of the opposing ABA captains was Edgar Eisenhower who was a brother of the golf-loving President, then in his last summer at the White House, but claimed to be a much better player. Safe in their fourball format and the heat and humidity of a Maryland August, the ABA easily won the match at Burning Tree by the embarrassing margin of 31 ½ – 1 ½, probably the Society's heaviest defeat. The American individual scratch prize winner modestly said: "Well I guess this proves we practise golf and the British practise law". The Society's Tommy Walmsley saved some pride by taking second place in the individual handicap event with a net 70 off his 15 handicap.

The match was again a success and the ABA suggested an annual fixture at their convention which the Society had to decline on the basis it would be impossible to raise a team to travel each year: after all, it was the first overseas trip by the Society since Robson Sadler had led a team to Dublin in 1913.

Since the first successful matches, there have been informal matches involving the ABA when it has held its conferences in London. The courses had to be chosen with care as the ABA as such was not allowed to play at any club which exercised any form of discrimination; even though many of the ABA members probably personally played at clubs such as Burning Tree, which was an all male club where women were turned away at the gates. One of the matches was at Sunningdale in 1971, again organised by Bobby Furber and captained by Bill Farrer, where the bar bill almost exceeded the green fees as the Americans tried out Kummel, a drink rarely seen away from traditional British golf clubs. There was also a game of slow fourballs at Wentworth in July 1985. Talk of a fixture against American golfers based in London never took off and the claret jug presented for the matches with the ABA was redesignated the Walmsley Cup and is now kept at Woking and played for each year in the match against the Bar.

But it was in 1961, the year after the Washington trip, that the continuing success of the Society was assured by the start of a more domestic fixture. The matches against the Writers to the Signet GC at Royal St George's and Muirfield, which also in the earlier years involved visits to the R&A, are described separately. This match meant the cementing of old friendships and the making of new ones in a way which is more easily achieved on a tour rather than one-off meetings and matches.

Francis Perkins: to many the essence of smoothness

At about the same time, the London base of the Society meant a further change. The links with the Law Society, which had existed since its foundation, effectively wound down on the founding of the nationally based Law Society Golf Club in 1962, promoted by Birmingham based solicitors, and the President of the Law Society ceased to be elected a Vice President of the Society after 1963. The Rules were however never changed and, even in the 21st century, contain the language about the President of the Law Society which, in 1922, caused the row between Rothwell Haslam and Trayton Kenward.

By now the younger members were actively running the Society. In addition to Bobby Furber, Francis Perkins had already been Captain in 1954 and remained a perennial presence in the Society, always dapper and courteous, and, to many, the essence of smoothness. Perhaps his calmness came from his dangerous and sensitive wartime minesweeping work for which he was awarded the DSC. He won many competitions, including the Stoneham Porringer for Clifford-Turner with Raymond Clifford-Turner.

His successor as Captain, Ben Hutchings, was a little older and a well regarded member of the Society and was later senior partner of Lovell, White and King. On being asked by Peter Morley-Jacob to amend an incorrectly completed standing order, he returned the form with the apology, "Cobblers' children are always the worst shod".

Peter Marriage was an imposing figure, sometimes even domineering. He was however one of the best of the post-war golfers, playing off 1 handicap at his best. Marriage was Captain in 1959 and later, as senior partner of Slaughter and May, did a great favour to the Society by effectively volunteering the services of the young Peter Morley-Jacob as Secretary, a post he took up in 1974. He took

some of the photographs in this book and also some in the Woking centenary history, *A Temple of Golf.*

Peter Marriage (left), one of the 1949 recruits, and Ray Gardner in 1963

Marriage's foursomes partner, Tommy Walmsley, was rather different and, even then, represented an old fashioned approach to the role of a City partner. He was charming and good with clients, some of whom he entertained royally, as indeed he did members of the Society. He was Captain in 1973 and a Vice President from 1978 until his untimely death in 1980. He started the tradition of the one Committee meeting a year being followed by a dinner, until recently at the Captain's expense, at a stroke ensuring full attendance. The Committee meeting when he was Captain was, rather dangerously, held in the Empress Restaurant and "closed in a convivial alcoholic haze with the members expressing appreciation to Mr Walmsley for his kind hospitality". Most importantly, he took many excellent photographs of the early matches against the Writers to the Signet.

In the 1960s the Society remained keen on good golf and quick golf. This was reinforced by good new recruits such as Don (known as "Horsey") Kerr who played off better than three and won at least four scratch prizes and was Captain in 1962. The previous year he had achieved that rarest of golfing feats, beating Dick Normand in the first playing of the Writers' match. John Parry-Jones, a Welsh international, was another good player who won three scratch prizes in the early 1960s and was Treasurer for 10 years from 1969. Playing in the top match, he probably had the privilege of hitting the first shot for LSGS in the fixture against the Writers.

Don (Horsey) Kerr, one of the better early post-war players

Handicaps were rigorously enforced and anybody over 18 was excluded. It was felt that the Meetings were sufficiently well attended and weaker players might hold up the speed of play. Chris James, later Captain and Treasurer before his premature death, was initially excluded from membership on handicap grounds: the minutes directed that the disappointment should be tempered by a "polite" letter, on the basis presumably that a person with a poor handicap might otherwise feel the subject of derision.

The policy of playing on the good heathland courses was maintained as was the commitment to foursomes golf. There was, however, a concession to the less expert with the introduction of stableford scoring for most competitions in the early 1960s, although the scratch prizes continued to be played for on a medal basis.

Leslie Nathanson was an important and well regarded figure in the London

Solicitors' GS as it went from strength to strength in the post-war period; he was Captain in 1961, at the start of the fixture against the Writers to the Signet, and was President from 1973 until shortly before his death in 1982. A keen tennis player in his youth, his later love of the good things of life, including good food and fine wine, particularly Burgundy, and port, was made sweeter by his experiences in the war.

Bob McGill playing out of a bunker at Muirfield in 1970 watched by a very smartly dressed caddy

As a young gunner lieutenant he had been captured in the North African desert and taken as a prisoner of war to Italy. Following the Italian armistice in 1943, his PoW camp had been recaptured by the Germans and on 11th September he and his fellow prisoners were on a train of cattle trucks in Modena about to be taken to Germany. Nathanson managed to slip away from the train and, helped by an Italian signalman who disguised him as a railway worker complete with red flag, managed to walk straight past the SS guards and out of the station. Six Englishmen were smuggled out of the station that day at great risk to the Italians who sheltered and fed them and, a little later, led them on an escape route over the Alps, which would eventually see 250 PoWs reach Switzerland. Leslie Nathanson ate many good meals but probably none tasted better than his first in Modena: "excellent pasta and the salad with dressing that was just right, and the rabbits cooked over the open fire so that their sides were golden brown. The bread was white and the red wine of Modena was good and plentiful...the [dolce] had real cream". Indeed such a meal was unobtainable in England in 1943. After the war there were happy and grateful reunions with the Italian helpers and Leslie Nathanson was the secretary of a committee which raised funds from ex-PoWs and others to build a Citta dei Ragazzi ("Boy's Town") to provide educational and recreational facilities for the young of Modena.

In the early 1950s, Leslie Nathanson founded Nabarro Nathanson with Felix Nabarro, who was also a member of the Society. Sadly, as with so many other firms, many years later the Nathanson name fell the victim of the fashion for shortening the names of law firms to give the impression of modern dynamism.

In his later years he adopted a patrician working pattern: his chauffeur, Carpenter, used to drive him to and from work in his Rolls Royce at a stately speed through Richmond Park. On the day before a Society meeting, Carpenter would drive down to the golf club where the meeting was to be held with the port from the Nathanson cellar so as to ensure it had settled and could be enjoyed to the full by all members at lunch the next day. On his death in 1982, he left all his remaining port to the Honourable Company of Edinburgh Golfers, which he had joined as a result of the friendships made following his successful captaincy of the first LSGS team to play the Writers to the Signet GC.

It was fitting that at a dinner in his honour, held by past Captains and committee members of the Society in June 1982 at Buck's Club, Leslie Nathanson and the other 14 attendees should consume 31 bottles between them, 12 of Champagne, 9 of Meursault 1978, 6 of Volnay 1976 (Jean Lefort) and 4 bottles of port (1966 Warre's). He was probably even more pleased the following month with a hole in one at the 16th at Woking in one of his last rounds of golf.

One of Leslie Nathanson' s great friends was Ray Gardner who spent more than 50 years with Gordon Dadds after joining the firm in 1932. He looked the part as a prosperous Mayfair lawyer, comfortable in a dinner jacket, and with his charming smile and quiet manner became a highly regarded divorce and society lawyer. He always drove a Bentley and his white golf shoes and cigarettes lent a slightly raffish air. But nobody ever had a bad word to say about him.

He was a prominent LSGS member and for many years turned out for most meetings and many matches. Gardner was Captain in 1972 and Vice President from 1980 to 1990 before becoming President from 1990 until his death in 1993. Although his keenness was never questioned, his golf was perhaps in the non-expert camp. Indeed, during a match against the Writers to the Signet, he achieved the rare feat of an airshot on the green, albeit on the 13th at Muirfield which has its own special terrors, even for more competent golfers. He did however once win the HCEG Captain's weekend at Muirfield.

Ray Gardner left the Society £3,000 in his will. Some of this legacy was spent on a trophy which is played for each year in the match against the Lloyd's Golf Club, which Gardner had run for many years with his son, Richard, as his opposite number until his death in 1988. Partly because Sir Richard Greenbury, the chairman of Marks and Spencer, had given the address at Gardner's memorial service, it was decided that the balance and other Society funds should be invested in Marks and Spencer shares, unfortunately not the best of timings as things turned out.

A salver presented to Ray Gardner by his partners at Gordon Dadds is now played for as the Captain's prize for the best aggregate score over the Autumn and Spring meetings.

After Bobby Furber retired as Secretary in 1963, there were three in relatively quick succession, Tony Nieland, Jack Hutchings and Gordon Toland, all from Lovell, White and King. In 1974 Peter Morley Jacob was elected Secretary and began a new period of administrative stability with only two secretaries in the next 29 years.

Ray Gardner (left) and Ben Hutchings, both important supporters of the Society

CHAPTER SIX

Memories of the first match against the Writers to the Signet GC

F R Furber

MY RECOLLECTION of the founding of the annual match against the Writers to the Signet is very clear. Leslie Nathanson, who had been a keen supporter of the London Solicitors' Golfing Society since before the War and was a very popular member, was to become Captain in May 1961. Committee meetings in the days when I was Secretary were often held after lunch and over port at the Law Society's Hall. At one of these meetings, in February 1961, Leslie Nathanson said he wanted to mark his forthcoming year of office by some special occasion.

It so happened that I had been glancing through the minute books and had noticed that C J Y (Jimmy) Dallmeyer, who was then an articled clerk in London, had become a member of the Society in April 1934 at a meeting chaired by his father R J Y Dallmeyer who was Captain that year. He also had the distinction of winning the scratch prize in his first Society meeting that summer at Walton Heath with a fine 75. As I knew Dallmeyer, a well known Wykehamist and Cambridge golfer, had moved to Edinburgh and become a Writer to the Signet, I suggested that I should contact him and find out if there was any chance of a match between the Society and the Writers. Leslie Nathanson immediately embraced the idea. We would suggest that the first match should be a two day affair at Sandwich where I had just become a member. I was later to discover that Royal St George's, with Charles Murray Smith, Vivian Pollock and others, was one of the breeding grounds of the Society. We of course hoped that a "return" would be offered the next year at Muirfield (where Jimmy Dallmeyer had already been Captain of the Honourable Company) and perhaps every third year the match might go to Lancashire or Yorkshire, although this has never happened.

By a most fortunate chance, when I spoke to Jimmy

Bobby Furber's note to Peter Marriage setting out the arrangements for the first match, including the lunch at the Coq d'Or

THE LONDON SOLICITORS' GOLFING SOCIETY

Hon. Secretary:
F. R. FURBER
Tel. MONarch 1211

11, OLD JEWRY,
LONDON, E.C.2

September, 1961.

Dear Peter

Match .v. The Writers to the Signet
Golf Club

An 18 a-side match has been arranged against the Writers to the Signet Golf Club on Saturday, 28th October at Royal St. Georges Golf Club, Sandwich.

This is a rather special occasion and it is anticipated that the return match next year will be at Muirfield, as the W.S. Club includes several past captains of the Honourable Company.

The Captain wishes to entertain the W.S. side to lunch at the Coq D'or, Stratton Street, on Friday, 27th October, and it is proposed to arrange transport by motor coach to Sandwich after lunch for the visitors and any one in our side who wishes to avail themselves of it.

The match on Saturday will be by foursomes all day. Accommodation has been booked at the Guilford Hotel for the nights of 27th and 28th October and there will be a dinner at the Guilford Hotel on the Saturday night (dinner jackets); we shall return to London after lunch on Sunday.

We shall be the "hosts" to the extent of paying the green fees and the cost of the dinner.

Can you let me know at the earliest possible moment whether you would like to play and also whether you will attend the lunch and travel down by coach, or otherwise.

Yours sincerely,

Bobby

P. Marriage Esq.,
18 Austin Friars,
E.C.2.

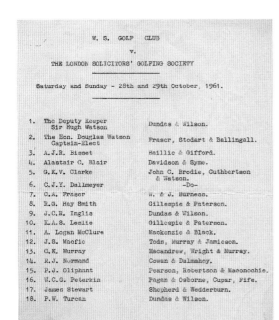

(left) The WSGC team sheet for the 1961 game

(right) Jimmy Dallmeyer. The record of his win at Walton Heath in the 1934 Summer meeting prompted the original contact with the Writers to the Signet GC

Dallmeyer on returning to the office he said he had just been attending a golf committee meeting – of the newly formed Writers to the Signet Golf Club – and the subject of possible fixtures was on the agenda. He was sure the WSGC would accept the challenge. Originally it was assumed that 12 a side would be sufficient for the opening game, but in the event 18 Scots came down for the match, mainly by train to Kings Cross.

Leslie Nathanson was determined that this first encounter should go off with a bang: accordingly he invited both teams to the old (and much lamented) Coq d'Or Restaurant in Stratton Street – one of Leslie's favourite haunts – before being transported by motor coach or car down to Sandwich. Shortly after 12.30 on Friday 27th October 1961 the first of many bottles of 1953 vintage champagne was poured in the Coq d'Or and the memorable first meeting with the WS team began and continued, as Leslie intended, with a splendid lunch which he paid for himself. It was particularly pleasing for Leslie Nathanson that his wartime friend and fellow officer, Douglas Watson, was captain-elect of the WSGC and they both said a few words at the lunch.

By the time the golf clubs and players were loaded into the motor coach and the waiting cars (including Leslie's sedate Rolls-Royce, driven by the imperturbable Carpenter – who doubled as a caddy), the sky had darkened. A cloudburst was encountered when we were leaving London on the old A2 winding through Dartford, Rochester and Gillingham as the motorway was still to come. A "comfort stop" at a pub beside the road was, needless to say, the occasion for drinks all round in the ancient hostelry below the level of the road – and showing signs of recent flooding from the rain.

F. R. Furber

27th October 1961
Inaugural Match
Writers to the Signet Golf Club
v
London Solicitors Golfing Society

at
Royal St. Georges
28th October 1961

MAYFAIR 7807-9   STRATTON STREET, PICCADILLY W.1.

Cocktails – Sherry

Champagne Charles Heidsieck

Chassagne Montrachet – Caillerette
original Bottling by Bachelet-Ramonet

Clos de la Roche 1949 en Magnum
original Bottling by Armand Rousseau

Taylor's Port 1927

La Grande Fine Champagne Cog
et Liqueurs

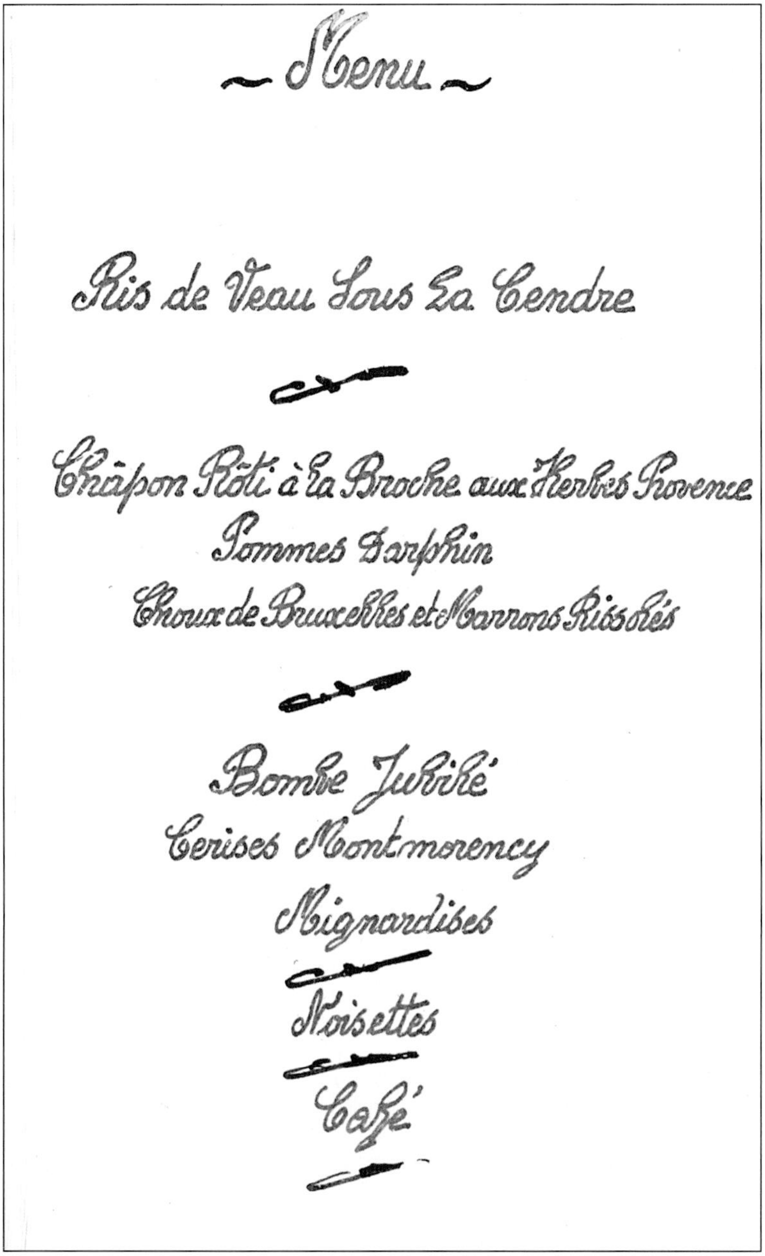

~ Menu ~

Ris de Veau Sous La Cendre

Chapon Rôti à La Broche aux Herbes Provence
Pommes Darphin
Choux de Bruxelles et Marrons Rissolés

Bombe Jubilé
Cerises Montmorency

Mignardises

Noisettes

Café

Occasionally a glimpse of an old menu, with wines no longer available, excites the imagination. Leslie Nathanson's lunch at the Coq d'Or started with vintage champagne, Charles Heidsieck 1953, which would then have been at its best. The white wine was Chassagne Montrachet, Les Caillerets 1959, Bachelet-Ramonet. Jean Bachelet was at the peak of his powers and would have coped well with the very hot summer of 1959, when Peter May, Cowdrey and Barrington were endlessly batting for England.

But the star of the show would be have been the red wine, Clos de la Roche 1949, Armand Rousseau; and in magnums. Clos de la Roche, a grand cru in Morey St Denis, is one of the best vineyards in Burgundy. Then, as now, Armand Rousseau was one of the best names and domaines in Burgundy. Rousseau had supplied most of the great restaurants in Paris in the 1930s and after the War he had begun acquiring his own parcels of land and led the way in domaine bottling and private selling. Clive Coates's magisterial *Cote d'Or* suggests that Armand Rousseau may not then have acquired his own parcels in Clos de la Roche but the menu says the wine was originally bottled by Armand Rousseau, probably from grapes grown by others.

About the year, 1949, and the greatness of the vintage there is no doubt. Clive Coates again: "This is the best vintage of them all, equal to 1945 or 1961 in Bordeaux. It contains wines of such perfect beauty and purity, that I have had to control myself not to weep with pleasure when I have tasted them... The 1949s are the epitome of Pinot Noir. Good structure, perfect harmony, generously fruity and of real intensity and breed. Everything is in place: glorious wines."

Afterwards, there were cigars and port, Taylor's 1929. Nobody in the world had a better lunch that day.

(top left) Sir Hugh Watson in a smoke filled bridge room

(top right) Leslie Nathanson (right) and Dick Normand at the Guilford Hotel

(bottom right) Charles Fraser (left) and Bobby Furber with Peter Marriage behind

Both sides stayed at the Guilford Hotel, a splendid Edwardian establishment in Sandwich Bay but now demolished. After dinner, as bridge was played and cigars smoked, Leslie Nathanson and I fixed the matches with Douglas Watson and Ramsay Bisset who was acting as secretary. The morning matches were played in vague order of playing ability and the afternoon pairings were more mixed, a practice that has continued, although that year the captains and secretaries played together.

The day of the match was fine, sunny and warm and the Society were 6 ½ – 2 ½ up at lunch and went on to win 12–6. Even Dick Normand, who was to play for the WSGC team for many years, was only able to win one of his games.

That evening we enjoyed the first of our annual black tie dinners at which Sir

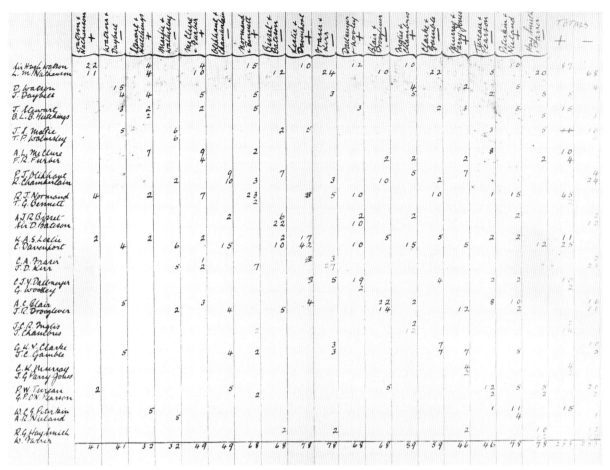

The sheet prepared by Jimmy Dallmeyer recording the bets in the 1961 dinner matches

Dingwall Bateson, our President and past President of the Law Society, accepted for the first time the silver rose bowl which had been presented by Leslie Nathanson. The bowl was named after Sir Hugh Watson, the Deputy Keeper of Her Majesty's Signet, who played in the first match and was one of the great characters of the early years. The dinner also saw the first announcing of the dinner matches, mixing the two teams, and there was wagering on the results according to Honourable Company rules with a designated Recorder, appropriately Jimmy Dallmeyer. The dinner matches have continued to be played the day after the match, although later on level terms rather than handicap.

In addition to the format many of the important faces of the WS team in the early years played in the first match including (in addition to those already mentioned) Charles Fraser, later to become the WSGC secretary, Alastair Blair, Logan McClure (who won both his opening games), RK Watson and Roger Inglis.

The following year, just as we had hoped, the return match took place at Muirfield and the fixture quickly became a very popular annual event.

CHAPTER SEVEN

The Baby Boom Generation Appears
1974 to 1987

WHEN PETER MORLEY-JACOB became Secretary in 1974 the national economic position was dire. The first great oil price rise in 1973 and stock market crash of 1973-74 had brought an immediate end to the Barber boom; the miners had been on strike for the second time in three years and a three day week had been in force to try and ensure electricity was available for at least part of the day. The Law Society Finals in 1972 and 74 were taken with power cuts interrupting progress. For those fortunate enough to be taking the exams there, the glass roof in Alexandra Palace gave some access to natural light. There were doubts as to whether the country was governable at all and it was assumed that it was only a matter of time before Paris or Frankfurt, or perhaps both, would replace London as Europe's leading financial centre.

For the London Solicitors' Golfing Society, the main effect was the inflation of the late 1970s. At the beginning of the 1970s golf was still a relatively cheap game; it was possible for those attending the College of Law in Guildford to have a six months student membership of Woking, West Hill or Worplesdon for about £5. In 1973, the total cost of the Spring meeting at the Addington was £4.25, including green fees, lunch and tea. Golf clubs then began to scramble to keep up with the effects of inflation. By 1977, when the Society moved the Spring meeting permanently to Woking, it was noted with concern that inflation had caused the cost of a day's golf, including lunch, at a LSGS meeting to rise to £10.50. Since then things have got worse and green fees for the casual visitor (those not playing with a member) have consistently outstripped inflation.

The London Solicitors' GS was also affected by the robber baron attempt by the brothers Nelson Bunker Hunt and Herbert Hunt to corner the world silver market in the 1970s. The price went from less than $2 per

Ray Gardner (left), Jack Drooglever and Bill Farrer (with moustache) in the bar of the Guilford Hotel, Sandwich in the 1960s

ounce to a peak of more than $50 per ounce. In 1968 the Stoneham Porringer, Ellis Cunliffe Vase and Sir Joseph Hood Cup had been valued together at £592. By 1978 the valuation of the Stoneham Porringer alone had risen to £2,500 and all the Society's trophies had to be revalued at considerable additional cost for insurance. By 1980, the height of the bubble, it was doubted whether the Society could continue to give silver spoons as prizes. Many fine pieces of silver, but fortunately not the Society's, were melted down for their bullion value.

The increase in inflation in the 1970s was reflected in the annual subscriptions. The initial subscription in 1904 was 5 shillings (25p), increasing to 10 shillings (50p) in 1920. This held for almost 50 years before an increase to £1 was made in 1968 followed by a major jump to £5 in 1981. The millennium was celebrated by an increase to £10 a year. The three increases from 1968 have involved members changing their standing orders, which has taken them years, or sometimes decades, with some benevolently or, more probably, forgetfully paying both the old and the new subscriptions.

For the solicitor in 1974, in all this change and turmoil, the mechanical tools of the profession had hardly changed since the founding of the London Solicitors' GS in 1904. Typewriters had been in common use since the 19th century, but it was only in the 1960s that electric typewriters began to be introduced and golf ball typewriters were the height of sophistication. Even then there was not yet any memory capacity and word processing was some years away. The telex and telegram had also been in use for many years but the need for upper case made them tiresome to read. The telephone, Lord Riddell's favourite means of communication, was the major development of the early part of the 20th century but in 1974 it was still relatively expensive, particularly for overseas calls, and only landlines were in use. Even the ability to make copies was strictly limited, photocopiers were primitive and only black and white, or worse, white on black. The circulars to Society members were "roneoed", involving a specially prepared master draft being hand turned on a machine with well inked rollers, with every turn of the handle producing one very wet copy of the page.

Few would then have guessed that this was the beginning of the end of the golden age of the solicitor and the legal secretary working closely together, the solicitor dictating and the secretary then typing letters and documents, for sending by post or by hand. As the primary means of communication in 1904, the post had been efficient: its long decline in frequency and reliability followed remorselessly from the introduction of each new and faster means of communication.

Dictation, an underrated skill and one that is dying as surely as the skill of a weaver using a water powered cotton jenny, had been made a little easier by the introduction of dictating machines, although many solicitors preferred to

Sunningdale has never been cheap but in 1971 the green fee was £3, marginally more than the lunch at £2.50

Peter Morley-Jacob at the gate to the Royal St George's garden in 1995

dictate directly to secretaries, now exclusively female, taking shorthand. Accuracy by both solicitor and secretary was essential as corrections were almost impossible without telltale smears of Tipp-Ex. In those days a PS was genuine and not a literary device and cc did indeed mean carbon copy. Even then, if the carbon paper was not properly used there was no copy.

Everything was done directly to paper, documents were amended by hand or sometimes by typewriter with longer riders typed up separately. Public documents were printed in the still traditional way of setting type. All of this made for admirable brevity: the sale of the business of Rolls Royce Motors in 1973, following the receivership of Rolls Royce, was just five pages long, a full flotation prospectus could be 8 or 10.

By the end of Peter Morley-Jacob's term as Secretary in 1987 this had changed with the introduction of the first fax machines (now themselves almost as obsolete as a typewriter) and word processing capability at the beginning of the 1980s. As every solicitor knows, documents began to get longer as, in a development or mutation of Parkinson's Law, the words expanded to fill the word processing capability available.

Societies and clubs, of course, change much more slowly as personalities ebb and flow. In 1974 most of the principal figures of the post-war Society were still active. There were many others. Bill Farrer was Captain in 1971 and Vice President from 1984 until his death in 2004. He was senior partner of Farrers and hid a shrewd brain behind a bluff exterior and a distinctly Dickensian harrumph as he began to speak.

Jack Watney at Sunningdale in 1971

The match against the Writers to the Signet was by now firmly established as the highlight of the Society's year although invitations to the team were carefully monitored and it did not appear on the fixture card until 1992. Partly in imitation of the Writers, the Society from 1974 had three Captains who served for two years instead of one. Jack Watney was Captain from 1974 to 1976 and celebrated in 1974 by winning the Stoneham Porringer for Masons with his son Adrian. Both father and son were Masters of the Mercers' Company. John Wilson, who followed him as Captain, founded the match against the East Anglian lawyers in the mid 1970s as described elsewhere and later, as a result of friendships made in the Writers' match, moved to Gullane where a gate in his boundary wall, like a portal in Philip Pullman's Dark Materials trilogy, gave direct access to Muirfield. John Goble, Captain from 1978 to 1980, was later senior partner of Herbert Smith and is renowned, rather like a star of screen and stage, for having splendid glossy hair that has not kept pace with his years.

All of these two year Captains were delightful men and great supporters of the Society, but the LSGS was lucky enough to have a growing crop of younger members coming through, some of whom were of the baby boom generation, and was able to revert to one year captaincies in 1980.

In addition, these young players were now dominating the meetings, just as the fresh young lawyers had done after the Second War. Indeed such was the dominance of the young golfing talent that there were to be no more scratch medals for the post-war generation after 1967, the year of the so-called summer of love.

Jeremy Caplan had joined the Society in 1965 and immediately made his mark. For some years before Peter Morley-Jacob became Secretary, the Society had been lax in making sure the cups were engraved with the names of the winners, or indeed returned by them. This was partially corrected in the mid 1970s but there are several missing years on a number of trophies, including from 1969 to 1976 on the Crocker Trophy, presented by Sir William Crocker in 1954, the prize for the best scratch score at the Spring meeting. Even without the missing years, Jeremy Caplan won 8 times between 1977 and 1992 and would, no doubt, have won many more in later years if the Spring meeting had not normally coincided with the Spring meeting of the R&A, as he reminds the Committee every year. In this period another good young player, Bruce Streather, managed four victories and, a third, Keith Gallon had two.

The Crocker Trophy: the prize for the scratch event at the Spring meeting at Woking

In the Autumn meeting the dominance of these three was similar with, again, Bruce Streather winning four scratch medals (for the American Bar Association Cup) and Keith Gallon winning two. Jeremy Caplan however may have won as many as 13 scratch medals at the Autumn meeting including 6 wins in a row between 1968 and 1973 and a 69 at New Zealand in 1983, the best recorded score in a Society meeting. It needs to be said that this record is uncertain as the results from 1968 to 1973 are not engraved on the cup; but in a 1978 letter to Peter Morley-Jacob, Caplan claimed at least four victories and "I think it may have been the lot".

Keith Gallon (left) and Jeremy Caplan in the mid 1970s – a poor time for shirt fashions

The ordinary players had to make do with the balance of the silverware, much of it dating back to the early days of the Society. As the Society's match play events fell away after the Second War, the splendid related cups (the Riddell Challenge Cup, Sir Joseph Hood Challenge Cup and Ellis Cunliffe Challenge Vase) were assigned to competitions at the Spring and Autumn meetings. Indeed there were so many trophies at these meetings they were rationed, like prizes at a children's party. It may be that this rationing helped Henry Johnson,

who with a handicap of 22 was fortunate to have been admitted as a member in 1936 (less than two years after the death of Lord Riddell). He won his four recorded trophies at a steady pace, with the first in 1952 and the latest in 1994, at the age of 78 and 58 years after he became a member. Although he was a rigorous enforcer of the return of cups for the Old Westminster golfers, it took him seven years to return the Riddell Challenge Cup he won in 1970, claiming that his wife had hidden it away from burglars in a cupboard under the bath. Henry Johnson is one of the oldest surviving members and came to the centenary dinner in 2004 when James Furber asked him to rise to general applause. A few moments later he was asleep; it is unclear whether this was the result of his exertions or the quality of Furber's speech.

The London Solicitors' Golfing Society was in good shape on its 75th anniversary in 1979: Peter Morley-Jacob was organising matters admirably and without the need for assistance from others. The Captains could relax in the knowledge that nothing would be required of them other than one committee meeting, a few words every now and then and a little hospitality; rather like a Doge in the Venetian Republic. And so it has remained ever since.

One of the secrets of a successful Secretary is for the administration not to be noticed. In this Peter Morley-Jacob was admirably successful both for the Society and, no doubt, for Slaughter and May where he was for many years the administration partner. His responsibilities included not only the Spring and Autumn meetings but also organising the matches against the Writers to the Signet and the East Anglian lawyers. Unfailingly courteous and modest, Peter Morley-Jacob would always agree to Leslie Nathanson's request for a visit to Surrey to discuss the Society's affairs and, on arrival, he would be asked: "What would you like first: a swim or a drink?".

Bruce Streather at the centenary dinner in 2004, many years after his first success in LSGS meetings but only three years after becoming the oldest winner of the President's Putter at Rye

New members would be looked out for at meetings and matches and offered a quiet word. Acts of generosity were performed without fuss. Members may have been drinking Kummels after lunch at matches and meetings for years without realising that Peter Morley-Jacob has paid for them, and the Committee only discovered accidentally that he had funded some new plinths for the Society's cups.

This was one of the times when the meetings were well attended and there was pressure on places, particularly at the Spring Meeting at Woking. There was a good blend of the young and the old, and even the older members were still, in the main, practising solicitors. The fashion for early retirement had not yet arrived, partly because the boom for legal services had not started and income tax was still at 60%. One of the reasons for the Society's continuing strength was the success of the Society's more dynamic members, many now in senior positions in the larger firms, in introducing younger members: Slaughter and May and Linklaters & Paines were particularly prominent and also Herbert Smith, Norton Rose Botterell and Roche and Clifford-Turner.

The 75th anniversary dinner in 1979 was held at the Law Society's Hall with a suitably 1970s menu of salmon mousse and beef wellington followed by black cherries marinated in brandy with praline ice cream. The cost was £13 a head and it was a great success with 129 members and guests, many from Scotland. The bit was between the teeth as further dinners were held in 1981 and 1984 (with the cherries and praline ice cream making a reprise in 1984), before the Society returned to a gap of five years or so between dinners: in other words a period when nobody could quite remember when the previous one had been held and everybody felt the need for another.

Sir George Riddell had first suggested in 1911 that lady guests should be invited to attend the dinners. The Committee had been uncertain about this initiative and had polled the members, 45 were in favour and 30 were against, but had then decided not to invite them anyhow because attendance was by then assured and "the closeness of the vote". There had been a further vote on ladies attending in 1929, also probably instigated by Lord Riddell, with 33 in favour and 23 against but again this had not resulted in attendance. Women had however come to the 50th anniversary dinner in 1954, but they were not invited to the later ones and so missed witty addresses in 1979 and 1981 by Stewart Lawson, later Captain of the R&A. He was made an honorary member of the Society in 1981 in appreciation of all he had done, including being a convivial host at the R&A.

In 1980 the young Jeremy Caplan was the first of the Captains for the reintroduced one year term. Even in the 21st century he continues to play with the extended shoulder turn and high follow through of the young golfer, perhaps the most stylish of swings among the Society's modern members. This quality has seen him win as many as 21 scratch medals at Society meetings and many other competitions over the years including the Oxford and Cambridge GS's President's Putter in 1986 and, perhaps most notably, the Worplesdon mixed foursomes with three different partners. Such was his continuing success that he was a Welsh triallist at a relatively advanced age. Voluble when excited, he can always be heard on social occasions. Rather like Herbert Taylor, his expert golfing predecessor in the LSGS, he has spent many golfing days away from his base in Jersey, some of them no doubt making sure he can justify his membership of 11 golf clubs. It is enviable to have to turn down a Society match because of a trip to Pine Valley.

Jeremy Caplan in 1994. He continues to have the well balanced finish of the younger man.

(left) Frank Donagh in 1971, with the luminous eyes of the young Paul Newman

(right) Chris James (facing) and Robin Burleigh in 1991. Chris James was initially rejected on handicap grounds but later became Captain and Treasurer

His successor as Captain in 1981 was Keith Gallon who similarly remains a good golfer, and a strong supporter of the Society, with a pleasantly old fashioned use of the knees through the ball. In his youth he won the Father and Son competition at West Hill and in 1979 won the Royal St George's Captain's Medal with a gross score of 149 (74+75), thus emulating the previous successes of Vivian Pollock. He has almost certainly played more matches than anybody else in the representative games against the solicitors from Scotland, East Anglia and Ireland.

Robin Burleigh, a Clifford-Turner partner, was Captain in 1985 and had been the first of the new young players to win a scratch medal, at the Spring meeting at Woking in 1968. Frank Donagh had preceded him as Captain in 1984 and was a good player, then with the luminous eyes of the young Paul Newman. Donagh was a partner of Herbert Oppenheimer whose Victorian offices, also occupied by Herbert Smith, had one of the last hydraulic lifts in the City. Clive Rumbelow, who was Captain a little later in 1989, was a Slaughter and May partner with the air of the classics schoolmaster. But he represented the future in the size of the head of his driver, his best club, even in the days of wooden woods.

By the 1980s the effort put in by the post war generation had paid off: there was a good blend of the young and the older members and the meetings were well attended and the matches firmly established.

CHAPTER EIGHT

The Great Storm of October 1987

"**D**ADDY, what did YOU do in the Great Storm?"
The answer for 40 Englishmen and Scots was: "I was playing golf". The match against the Writers to the Signet GC is played in October, timed to catch the equinoxal depressions, perhaps to give more interest to the golf. As Mr Anderson, the former steward at Royal St George's once said: "Do you really like playing at this time of year in the wind and rain?". In 1987 the timing was more expert than normal. The match was played at Sandwich on Thursday 15th October, the eve of the Great Storm. The afternoon was very wet with the wind getting up; but it was unpleasant rather than unplayable, even though some gave up early. Peter Millar's caddy refused to go on and walked in from the 9th, saying "You're all mad", but Millar carried his clubs in the rain for an eventual WSGC win with Neil Crichton.

That evening the London Solicitors' GS members were relaxing in the warm glow of victory in the old internal dining room of the Bell Hotel in Sandwich, a somewhat grim room with no exposure to the outside and therefore no sense of the gathering storm. Brendan Lynch for many years arrived for the fixture freshly tanned from the Caribbean. He had famously been no less than an Eisenhower Trophy competitor for the Bahamas in 1974 although, rather like Dorian Gray, his 5 handicap never changed with the passing years. That evening he was asked by Chris James, without warning, to say grace before dinner. He quickly replied, moving from the sacred to the practical: "Oh Lord God above, give us the power to shift this lot in half an hour". Chris James and Ewen Cameron, the Captains, gave speeches true to their own characters.

After dinner the players crammed into the tiny back bar of the Bell, now the hotel offices, and carried

The dinner before the Great Storm. From left, Peter Younie (back), George Russell, Jeremy Caplan, Peter Morley-Jacob and Brendan Lynch

3 BALLS + 4 BALLS
MAY ONLY
BE PLAYED WITH
THE
SECRETARY'S
PERMISSION
THEY MUST GIVE WAY TO
SINGLES AND FOURSOMES

on drinking, as round after round was bought. Jonathan Chalton and Anthony Surtees were playing bridge, perhaps against Dick Normand, if he was able to find a partner who could handle the flinty stare of that most competitive of players. Bill Richards and Nigel Watt, both sporting buffs, were testing each other on Brechin City's away record in the late 1950s. Spencer Patrick was probably giving Neil Crichton his annual reminder how, on being roughly challenged to do so, he had outdriven him at the 10th in the 1983 dinner match. Almost certainly nobody listened to Michael Fish's famous forecast that night, warning of winds but not a hurricane. After all, everybody knew the dinner matches were sure to be played the next day in any event.

At about 1am Sandwich was hit with the full force of the biggest storm to hit England since 1703; 5 people died in Kent alone and 15 million trees were blown down in southern England. One fine tree, still in full leaf just outside the Bell, began to move ominously. Ray Gardner's Bentley was parked underneath and he was woken and asked if he wanted to move it. He tossed the keys to the porter and said, "You move it". Luckily it was moved, and the tree came down a little later, blocking the road in front of the hotel. Rubbish bins and anything else that was loose was being blown down the street outside the hotel at head height and roof tiles were hurtling into parked cars. Peter Morley-Jacob and others were woken by the noise of the wind and the crashes and retreated, huddled in blankets, to the ground floor for safety where the manager's wife supplied them with cups of tea. Others slept peacefully through the whole of the storm and were bemused to see the devastation the next morning, with broken tiles and other debris scattered over the streets, and to find there was no power or hot water in the hotel. Peter Younie woke to find that the whole of

The Bell Hotel, the morning after
the Great Storm. October 1987
was not a good time to have
planned roof works in Sandwich

Clive Rumbelow "struck down" in
the rubble in the Bell Hotel

the plaster ceiling in his bathroom had come down in the night without disturbing him.

James Furber, as a junior member in his first match, had been given an attic bedroom. He woke to a great crash and, assuming the Scots were energetically re-enacting the sack of the English baggage train after Bannockburn, he went back to sleep, vaguely worrying about his share of the damage. He woke in the morning to find that a chimney stack had fallen through the flat roof outside his bedroom and blocked the corridor.

There was no question of not trying to play golf but getting to the course was difficult as every other tree appeared to be down. Some, including Jeremy Caplan and Stephen Barnard, walked to the club carrying clubs and bags, climbing over the trees lying across the road. The majority taking a more sensible approach suggested by Chris James, found a treeless way to Deal passable by car and then came back to Royal St George's over the old coast road.

The club was open even though there had been substantial damage, with virtually all the tiles peeled off the back of the pro's shop, like a pack of cards. The damage was even greater at the old Prince's clubhouse where a chimney stack had fallen through the roof. The course was surprisingly playable in still very windy but warmish conditions, although all the fairways were covered in hay blown in from the surrounding farmland and every shelter had been blown away. The flagsticks however remained in the holes. Even though there was no electricity, the staff still managed to produce a fine oxtail stew. Indeed, it was only as the players drove back to London that the enormity of the damage became clear as the destruction of London plane trees had made south London almost impassable. But some of the Society members and the Scots still

*Jeremy Caplan driving off the 1st
tee at Muirfield in 1984 into the
gathering storm*

*Maxwell Ferguson taking
pre-emptive action in 1984*

managed to play the next day at the Addington, that most tree lined of courses, and so probably became the only people in southern England to play on each of the Thursday, Friday and Saturday of that week. The Addington fairways were half their normal width in places but a free drop was allowed for a ball finishing in a fallen tree.

Royal St George's would, of course, have been completely unplayable if the Great Storm had arrived during the day and the wind on the course on Thursday and Friday was, somewhat surprisingly, not as fierce as it had been at Muirfield in 1984. This was the only time that the match has been abandoned at lunch because of wind and rain, with the Scots winning thanks, in part, to some judiciously negotiated halves or abandonments as the softer or perhaps less weather beaten English made for the clubhouse to escape the storm. In 1984, for those starting at the 10th, the exposed 5th and 7th greens were almost unplayable, with the knowledge that a putt, once started, had to go in the hole or end in a bunker. For Dick Normand there was no question of a half or a concession even for a man in his seventies, except by the other side, and he played all 18 holes in the worst of the weather to secure a win. That lunchtime there was even more laughter than normal; a sign of hypothermia narrowly averted.

CHAPTER NINE

The End of the Century
1987 to 2004

N 1987 PETER MORLEY-JACOB's long term as Secretary came to an end; he had ill-advisedly failed to identify his successor in 1984 when he was Captain, and had had to serve another three years. James Furber was to serve even longer, until just before the centenary of the London Solicitors' Golfing Society in 2004. As Bobby Furber's son, this was an unusual example of a dynasty operating successfully with Furber senior overseeing matters as President until 1990, when Ray Gardner took over. A party at Farrer & Co to mark Bobby Furber's retirement as President saw a gathering of most of the surviving post-war generation. By 2004 at least one Furber had been on the Committee for each of the preceding 50 years and this record continues.

The 29 years of administrative stability of the Morley-Jacob/Furber secretariat were in sharp contrast to the changes in the solicitors' world. The fax and word processor were transforming the way work was done. At first this was a matter of amazement. Primo Levi wrote in 1985: "Two years ago, I bought myself a word processor, that is, a writing tool that returns automatically at the end of a line and makes it possible to insert, cancel, instantaneously change words or

(left) A dinner at Bubbs after the 1989 Committee meeting. From left, Bobby Furber, Barrie Lloyd (obscured), Peter Morley-Jacob, James Furber, John Hargrove, Bill Richards and Clive Rumbelow

(right) Peter Morley-Jacob and James Furber, the longest serving Secretaries of recent years, compare notes in 2010. Their firms, Slaughter and May and Farrer & Co, have been great supporters of the Society

entire sentences; in brief makes it possible to achieve in one leap a finished document, clean, without insertions or corrections". All of this is now old hat and has always been taken for granted by anybody born after 1970.

But this was just the beginning and the changes accelerated on the introduction of email a decade later: in just a few years every solicitor was behind a screen and needing to cope with the new technology. Mobile phones and, later, Blackberries meant that solicitors were always available for clients who were expecting a faster and faster service with every passing year. The Big Bang had taken place in the City in 1986 and all professions were under the scrutiny of Mrs Thatcher's government which was about to move on to the utility companies as part of its privatisation programme, involving some of the biggest jobs ever to be undertaken in the City. 1987 also saw the merger of the rapidly expanding Clifford-Turner and Coward Chance to form Clifford Chance, perhaps the most significant of all law firm mergers. The globalisation of the financial services industry and the law firms was about to begin in earnest. The result, which was completely unforeseen in 1974 when Peter Morley-Jacob took over as Secretary, was that by 2008 four of the six largest law firms in the world, by global revenues, had their headquarters in London.

As computers, mobile phones and other electronic equipment shrank and became more efficient, with smaller always being better, lawyers went the other way and worked harder as documents got longer and clients' expectations greater. No longer could a solicitor put a letter in the post knowing there would be no response for a couple of days: and no longer was a quiet game of golf possible without the risk of a client noticing or bothering. Increasingly, mid-week days of golf became more difficult to arrange and, like many other societies, those attending the Society's matches and meetings gradually began to be older or retired.

One active member who was certainly older and retired was Eric Swatton Brooks who was born in 1907 but in 1987 was still on the Solicitors' Roll. He won the Sir Joseph Hood Cup in 1930, which was then the prize for the Spring knock-out, the Society's oldest event, and he won it three more times in its modern format. His best years were the end of the 1930s when he won three scratch gold medals in a row at the Summer meeting - in 1938 with a fine score of 76 at the Addington. That afternoon he also won the foursomes with Gordon Petch, and he repeated the morning and afternoon double the following year at West Hill, the last LSGS meeting for 8 years. Brooks was good enough 48 years later to have won the Riddell Challenge Cup on the morning of James Furber's election as Secretary and was the last winner personally to remember the donor of the cup. In 1988 he won his final event, the Armada Dish, at the age of 80, more than 58 years after his first Society success. Here he had help, and he must have

been delighted with Leslie Nathanson's stipulation, when he gave the dish in 1974, that a competitor is entitled to add ½ a point to the stableford score for every year over 55. Eric Brooks, who was still a good player, duly won the Armada Dish 7 times, and in 1988 stood on the first tee with 13 points already in the bag.

James Furber is a believer in the best of traditions and is now senior partner of Farrer & Co, one of the more traditional law firms. "This is not a man who eats sandwiches for lunch", wrote a member proposing James for his club, and this was certainly not said in approval of Gordon Gekko's comment in the late 1980s about lunch being for wimps. James helped to ensure the Society remained true to its long standing ways during his term of office. Perhaps not one of the Society's galacticos on the course, James Furber can be relied upon to be better than scratch at lunch with his wit and droll comments.

But the London Solicitors' GS could not be complacent. As the introduction of new recruits by the older members declined and there was less time for golf, the membership by the late 1980s was less than 200, far fewer than the 363 members in 1935. Just as happened in the early 1920s and in the late 1940s, there were increasing worries about the lack of younger members. In 1987, a requirement was introduced that one of the competitors in the inter-firm competition for the Liberty Bowl at the Spring Meeting should be under 35 (although this was raised to under 45 in 2005). This requirement for youthful support has helped James Furber to a record 5 wins in the Liberty Bowl, in its various forms. These concerns for younger members continue to the present in an age of increasing demands on time from clients and families. Sometimes a promising young player bursts onto the scene only to vanish on promotion, changing firms or moving out of London. Those who have emerged and remained active from this

Frank Donagh plays out of the difficult bunker to the left of the 8th green at Royal St George's

period include Andrew Dixon, who once lost the sole of his golf shoe at Aldeburgh, Mark Clark, capable of spectacular golf shots, and Jeremy Gordon. On the other hand, some members appear at a more mature age, rather like the old Stoke football team or the recent AC Milan: examples are Arfon Jones and Nigel Bennett.

From time to time there has been discussion as to whether European and other lawyers should be allowed. A sensible proposal from the Committee to allow the admission of registered foreign lawyers, resident in London and working in a London firm of solicitors, was however rejected by members at the 2002 annual meeting. The increase in the number of women members has also been slow since Mrs M Satchell became the first female member at the time of the major recruitment drive in 1949. Unlike some other golfing societies and clubs there has however never been a policy of not admitting women. Mrs Satchell and her sister Mrs Joll, both county players, regularly played in the Society meetings in the 1950s and, not surprisingly, were popular partners in the afternoon foursomes. Jo Rickard became the first female committee member in 1990, followed later by Eleanor (Ellie) Evans. They have both been winners of the Sir Joseph Hood Cup and Ellie Evans is a match manager.

As the 20th century drew to a close, James Furber's notes to members on what could or could not be done with mobile phones, or worn or not worn, on the course or the clubhouse at the meetings became more and more elaborate. Golf club committees tend, like First World War generals, to be fighting the previous war in their efforts to ensure that everybody dresses just like themselves, without account of age. The women are more varied and subtle in their dress, which tends to mean dress codes are mainly aimed at the men. A major problem is that, left to themselves, male golfers often have dubious dress sense. This was

Golfers
who study their Dress.

SPEND an hour near a Golf tee on a busy day—it is astonishing the Coats affected by many players.

There come along old—shabby—disreputable—worn-out jackets one would not allow one's gardener to wear.

Then the no-pretence-at-fitting coats that look like badly-made shirts.

Then Norfolks, minus the pleats, or with pleats where they should be minus, and bulging shoulders with the appearance of broken blisters.

Still amongst them you will see many—very many—well dressed men, and if you enquire you will generally find that the suit is a "Burberry."

The best players invariably exhibit correct form in play, not only because it looks best but because it ensures the best results. So with the coat, elegance and taste will help the Golfer, and freedom can be got without resorting to monstrous devices.

30 to 33, Haymarket, LONDON, and BASINGSTOKE.

BURBERRYS,

Golf fashion in 1910

Golf fashion in 2010

(top left) In 1910 golfers were expected to be better dressed than their gardeners

(bottom left) John Rink (right) looks pleased with his pink shorts at a centenary event. Arfon Jones, also in shorts, is sensibly avoiding the camera

(top right) Herbert Taylor looking immaculate in 1911 as the winner of the London Amateur Four-somes. The spats sometimes had a practical purpose in dealing with the mud on low lying London courses

(bottom right) Martyn Gowar making a fashion statement at Rye not helped by Nick Faldo's first Open Championship win, also in 1987, and his subsequent clothing endorsements, which spawned ten thousand diamond spangled jerseys.

Every photograph before the First War shows Society members wearing jackets, ties and plus-fours, with HE Taylor, the Amateur Championship finalist, looking particularly elegant. The Burberry advertisement has a suitable exhortation to golfers: "Spend an hour near a Golf tee on a busy day – it is astonishing the Coats affected by many players. There come along old – shabby – disreputable – worn-out jackets one would not allow one's gardener to wear." Things began to slip in golfing fashion after the First War, with the hat and jacket the first to go and the tie following later. Lord Riddell, however, never wavered and wore a bowler in the Daimler to Walton Heath, only changing to a cap on the course. Bernard Darwin also noted that Riddell never played in what would be termed golfing clothes, but sober-suited with a stiff white collar.

When Henry Cotton had his great 65 at Royal St George's in the second round of the Open in 1934, which finally ended a long period of US dominance, he was still wearing plus fours but with a jersey in place of a jacket (for many a cardigan was a replacement) and was hatless.

After the Second War, things became more informal although with a still rigid internal fashion: after all nobody other than golfers or muggers wears white shoes. Edward, Prince of Wales, whose taste was doubtful on many matters, had previously led the way with two tone golf shoes which unfortunately can still be seen on the course. The nadir of golfing fashion probably came in the 1970s and 80s, with a particular weakness for loud trousers and ill fitting shirts, in both cases untouched by natural fabrics.

Some of the Society's members have tried to maintain the old standards. James Furber himself is often traditionally dressed in brown tweed plus-fours with matching jacket made of exemplary heavy material, capable of raising a good sweat even on the coldest day. Anthony Surtees is always immaculately turned out; a model of what good tailoring can achieve. His tailor has however had occasionally to warn him of an impending increase in measurement by the discreet euphemism: "I see sir is a little stronger in the body this time".

Thomas Fenwick, the founding Secretary, is photographed in the first game at Deal as if he is about to invade Russia, such is the weight of his clothing and the stoutness of his boots. He would surely be as astonished as the Burberry man at the 21st century fashion for middle aged men wanting to go back to childhood by wearing shorts on the golf course, with bare knees showing. Not only that but Fenwick's two most recent successors as Secretary, Chris Millerchip and Adam Walker, are among those who have been seen to have succumbed.

Anthony Surtees's immaculate dressing is alas not matched by a conventional swing. Like Lord Riddell, his stance, with the right foot well back, is alarming to new partners but effective. Indeed he got better and better after he was Captain in 1982, winning the scratch medal at the Spring meeting in 1984 and, 20 years later, in 2004.

In the early days of the Society, the individual prizes were valuable and were sometimes worth more than the challenge cups which were only held by the winners for a year. Recently, the grandeur of these trophies has been more than sufficient for the winners. Gambling has moved in the course of a century from being an indulgence of the wealthy to an occupation primarily for those who can least afford it. There was huge gambling in the early days of golf and Harold Hilton, for example, records much wagering during amateur events including the Amateur Championship. In the 1970s playing for a "wrapped" ball, probably a Dunlop 65 (named after Cotton's great round) in its distinctive black wrapping, was more common. By the end of the century, the sweepstake had been abandoned at the Society's meetings: it was an administrative burden and produced very little for the winner.

Anthony Surtees, always well turned out, practising in 1996. Playing round his left foot, the ball would have finished in the camera's view

Although the Society dinners have been less frequent in recent years they have become grander, with the venue moving from the Law Society's Hall to the Mercers' Hall in 1991 and then to Middle Temple Hall in 1999 and for the centenary dinner in 2004. The cost also increased with the Mercers' dinner costing £67.50 per head, perhaps because the members were enjoying Chateau Grand Puy Lacoste 1976. They also enjoyed Peter Morley-Jacob's grace:

> "For food, for drink, for course, for links,
> For friendship, challenge and fair play,
> For putts and drives (less yips and shanks);
> For these, oh Lord, we give you thanks."

Adrian Watney was the Master of the Mercers' Company that year and gave a polished speech. He had been Captain in 1986 and he would be the first to admit his charm and infectious laugh are superior to his golf. Many people have held office for long periods with a light hand on the tiller but perhaps none with such a gossamer touch as Adrian Watney in his role as Fixture Secretary, which he held for 29 years from 1980 to 2009.

He was greeted rudely at a Committee meeting in the centenary year as the minutes reveal: "The Committee were delighted to greet Mr Watney – attending his first Committee meeting since 1996 (when his car, a Triumph Stag, had been towed away by the police). Mr Watney was characteristically shameless but nevertheless offered his resignation as he could not recall arranging any fixtures since his appointment. The Committee agreed that the role was somewhat redundant but refused to accept his resignation on the basis that he was therefore the perfect man for the job." This was a little unfair as Watney, even excluding his diligent attendance in his years as Captain and Vice Captain, had attended as many as seven Committee meetings in his 29 years, three of them in an industrious spell in the early 1990s.

Barrie Lloyd, Adrian Watney's partner at Masons, also held office as Treasurer for many years, from 1985 to 2006 and was also Captain in 1991. Again, the laugh and the cries of "Hello matey" are as distinctive as the swing, a hunched swoop at the ball which can be surprisingly effective. He also made the decision, on retiring, to join the English cricketing Barmy Army, something only to be recommended to those with serious masochistic tendencies. He has done much for the London Solicitors' Golfing Society, including organising several dinners.

Both Barrie Lloyd and Adrian Watney were able to take advantage of the generous provision in the Masons' partnership agreement, which allowed for days for golf not to count as holiday, without specifying the number of days. Other members of the Society, taking advantage of the new rules on continuing professional development, are rumoured to have resorted to striking days through in the office diary with "on a course" as the explanation.

The one Committee meeting a year rule (an excellent discipline) has been in place for many years and the meeting is usually well attended with a dinner afterwards. In recent years, the match managers, who do much of the work of the Society, have been invited to the dinner. It is sensible to make suitable preparations for these meetings, as the committee members are likely to agree with Kingsley Amis that the least welcome five words in the English language are: "Shall we go straight in?", with "A bottle of House Red?" a close second. The minutes recall however that over-exuberance on the catering was shown at Herbert Smith in 2000 where "for a meeting stated to be for 9 people, 6 large bowls of salty comestibles had been provided together with 6 bottles of champagne and 6 of white burgundy and 7 (all opened) of Rioja". The dinner itself was elsewhere.

The 18th green at Woking in 1904, two years before LSGS's first visit, with fields and farm buildings on the other side of the pond

As the end of the Society's first century approached, many of the matches and meetings had developed rituals that seemed to have been in place from the beginning. Although the Spring meeting has only been at Woking on a permanent basis since 1977, it is now hard to imagine it elsewhere. There is always a good attendance for the Spring meeting, partly because of the anticipation of a warm spring day and the chance to have a better golfing year; by the autumn the hope has usually evaporated. Woking is a club which is home to many lawyers, both barristers and solicitors, and LSGS's match against the Bar, first played at Woking in 1906, is the longest standing in the club's records. LSGS has often entered a team for the club's long established Alba Trophy, a scratch foursomes competition. The Society helped in the purchase of chairs for the club's centenary in 1993 and, in partial thanks for the club's hospitality, Tony Riley, the past Secretary, was elected an honorary life member of LSGS the following year.

Society members like to go to clubs beginning with W and during this period the Autumn meeting settled into a rhythm of Walton Heath, Worplesdon and Royal Wimbledon, with Royal Ashdown Forest as an exception to the Ws, to complement the Spring meeting at Woking.

Walton Heath remains unique in having been owned by a Society member, George Riddell, for the first 30 years of the Society's existence and LSGS has been playing there since 1906. In the 1930s, as described earlier, the Summer meetings at Walton were the highlight of the Society's year.

Even before Worplesdon opened, Herbert Taylor, in June 1908, made enquiries about a Society meeting on what "promised to be links of a very high class". Sadly, this appears not to have happened as the course was not yet ready,

Society members framed by Woking's wisteria after the 1995 AGM. John Hargrove, the new Captain, is receiving the Captain's putter from Philip Langford. Jo Rickard, the first female committee member and trophy winner, stands to the left

otherwise the Society might have been the first visitors. Taylor, however, joined, apparently as Worplesdon's lowest handicap founder member, as did Vivian Pollock. Taylor came second in the first Worplesdon medal in 1909, and won the following year with a 79. Perhaps this was the time he won two scratch medals on the same day, at Mid-Surrey in the morning and Worplesdon in the afternoon. Since the Second War, LSGS captains of Worplesdon have included Cyril Davenport, Don (Horsey) Kerr and Peter Marriage and, very recently, Barrie Lloyd and Jeremy Caplan.

Royal Wimbledon's proximity to central London has meant it has always had strong connections with the Society with a recent flurry of LSGS members, including Julian Walton, John Rink, Steven Turnbull and Andrew Barrow, holding the Royal Wimbledon captaincy.

Royal Ashdown Forest's connections are also longstanding. James Beale was an early captain and presented the Standen Cup which was won for the first time by Horace Hutchinson. Francis Perkins was also captain of Ashdown. Gordon Petch was both Captain and President of both club and Society and there was a well publicised LSGS meeting at Royal Ashdown Forest in 1972 for Gordon Petch's final day as President of the Society.

CHAPTER TEN

Matches against Societies

T HE MATCHES AGAINST other societies are these days played on a friendly basis, normally 36 holes of foursomes with a good lunch, where geniality is more important than the result. This was not always so, particularly in the golden age of the profession based golfing society before the First World War when great pride was attached to getting out the strongest sides. Bernard Darwin, commenting on golfing societies in this period, singled out the Bar, the Solicitors, the Stock Exchange and the Press. Each of them would expect to have at least one international in their side for important representative games, as mentioned in more detail in Chapter 1 and the London Solicitors' GS's best players, Herbert Taylor and Vivian Pollock, usually got up the Society's teams. Amateur golf at the highest level before the First War involved relatively few players and the total number of international golfers was tiny as the first amateur international match, between England and Scotland, had only taken place two years before the formation of the Society. But even the best of the golfing societies would not have been able to cope with a full strength Hoylake side including John Ball, Harold Hilton, Jack Graham, Charles Dick and others; the best club team in the history of amateur golf.

The matches mentioned below are those with fixtures in 2010. The matches against the Writers to the Signet GC and the East Anglian lawyers are covered later.

Long before the golf glove became fashionable, A H Davidson, for the solicitors, wore two in the 1904 game at Deal against the Bar

Bar and Bench

The newly formed Bar Golfing Society's first match in March 1904 is of particular importance as it led directly to the founding of the Society later that month. The win, on handicap, by the unofficial team of solicitors was avenged the next year in a scratch match when the Bar put out a very strong side at Royal St George's, containing three expert Scottish golfers. The Society, however, had marginally the better of the remaining competitive pre-war games, all of which

The front cover of Golfing in March 1904. The activities of golfing societies were widely reported in the Edwardian golden age

GOLFING.

VOL. XVIII. No. 456   MARCH 17, 1904.   ONE PENNY.

Barristers v. Solicitors at Deal.

MR. E. MARSHALL HALL, K.C., M.P., AT THE FIRST TEE.   MR. F. E. F. FAREBROTHER PUTTING.

MR. T. C. FENWICK DRIVING FROM THE THIRD TEE.

PLAY ON THE SIXTH GREEN.   *Photos by Baker & Dixon.*

were played at Woking. There was a particularly impressive top foursomes match in 1907 when Harold Beveridge and Bernard Darwin beat Herbert Taylor and Vivian Pollock. Pollock joined Darwin in playing for England in 1908 against a Scots team which included Beveridge. Taylor had to wait until 1911 for his English cap. After the resumption of the fixture in 1920, the matches became friendlier and were played at a number of courses with a slight advantage to the Bar.

The players in the centenary match against the Bar at Woking. Standing (from left) Barrie Lloyd, Tim Saloman, Martyn Gowar, John Davies, Nigel Wilkinson, Graham Dunning, Mark Shaw, Philip Langford, Roger Davies, Keith Gallon, Anthony Surtees and Tim Charlton. Middle, Michael Stephens, John Hargrove, Sir Roger Buckley, Richard Anelay, Ellie Evans, Ian Goldie and Jonathan Chalton. Front, Alastair Hodge, Michael Warren, Timothy Cray, Richard Grandison, Chris Millerchip and Jeremy Caplan

The Bar felt the effect of the young and enthusiastic new recruits in 1949, including Bobby Furber and Peter Marriage, when the Society recorded its best win of 7-1, as the match returned permanently to Woking. The two societies separately entertained the American Bar Association in 1957 and then combined to visit Washington in 1960 for a return fixture.

Although the records are not complete, LSGS has probably played more matches against the Bar than against any other society, with the Bar (more recently the Bar and Bench) holding the advantage in wins. In 2004 there was a dinner at Slaughter and May hosted by Richard Grandison, who for many years has been the match manager, and Ian Goldie. In the centenary match the following day, played in sunshine at Woking, the Bar and Bench pulled away after lunch, as has become traditional, to enable Richard Anelay, the match manager for the Bar, to receive the claret jug trophy, which had been presented by LSGS in 1980 in memory of Tommy Walmsley.

Ladies Legal

The Ladies' Legal Golf Association was founded in 1913, for the female relatives of judges, barristers, solicitors, bar students and articled clerks. A driving force in the formation was Mabel Stringer, a golf correspondent and a towering figure in the early days of the organisation of ladies' golf, who was also closely involved in the formation of other ladies' golfing associations, including those linked to the medical profession and Parliamentarians. She was known as "Auntie Mabel", a term coined by Cecil Leitch, a great early ladies' champion. Leitch had given a boost to ladies' golf, which was fast becoming fashionable, by beating Harold Hilton in a well publicised 72 hole match in 1910 at Walton Heath and Sunningdale in front of several thousand unruly spectators. She also beat Herbert Taylor 3 and 2 during a high profile 1911 Gentlemen v Ladies match at Stoke Poges, receiving a shot on each odd numbered hole.

Cecil Leitch playing from a bunker at Stoke Poges during the Ladies v Gentlemen match in 1911. She beat Herbert Taylor 3 and 2, receiving a shot on every odd hole

The record of the first game against the Ladies' Legal Golf Association in 1913, with the ladies receiving an additional 10 shots on top of handicap

At this time women were not eligible to join the Society as the legal profession was still closed to them and LSGS supported the formation of the Ladies' Legal. At the suggestion of Cyril Plummer, who was Captain of the Society in 1907 and whose wife was a founder member of the Ladies' Legal, the Society decided to give a cup to be played for at the Association's inaugural meeting. The Ladies' Legal preferred a Challenge Bowl and a silver rose bowl was procured for £6 15 shillings, rather more than the £5 budgeted, of a "handsome ornate design on a large ebony plinth". The Challenge Bowl was won for the first time by Mrs Rosalind Church Bliss, who appropriately was the first Captain of the Association, at the first Ladies' Legal golf meeting at Northwood in June 1913.

The Captain of the London Solicitors' GS (Litton Taylor) raised the strong team which played the first match against the Ladies' Legal at Hanger Hill on 2nd July 1913, with the Society winning 7-3 despite giving a somewhat embarrassing 10 additional shots on top of handicap in each game. Victor Longstaffe, playing top for LSGS that day, was fond of golf against ladies and had already achieved fame in 1910 by beating Cecil Leitch at Aldeburgh, although he had only given her 5 shots a round compared with the 9 shots she received from Hilton and Tayor.

Thereafter, the match has been one of the most regularly played and was one of the first to be re-introduced after the War. Throughout the 1920s and 30s, there was some confusion as to whether the Society should bear the ladies' green fees and other expenses and at one stage the match organiser was asked by the Committee to get prior approval before incurring expense. These days the Ladies' Legal pay their own way but the discussions on handicap and the number of additional shots still continue; particularly sensitive with two ladies playing together.

In the 1980s the match was 36 holes at West Sussex but more recently it has involved a late afternoon round of foursomes at Royal Wimbledon followed by supper. John Hargrove organised the match for many years and, with Julian Walton, presented some coasters as a prize for the match. Jonathan Chalton, energetically taking over from the younger man, has in recent years made the match arrangements with Gillie Barratt.

The Ada L. Abady Trophy

The Abady Trophy is a more traditional foursomes match with a man and a woman on each side and has been played since the 1950s, appropriately at Woking (that home of lawyers' golf, both barristers and solicitors), between LSGS and members of the Ladies' Legal who derive their membership through solic-

A gathering of Abady Cup players at Woking

Mrs Abady at Stanmore in 1922. She played in the 1920s in matches between ladies associated with the Bar and those associated with solicitors

itors and the Bar GS and members of Ladies' Legal who can trace their membership to the Bar. Here the well recorded results point firmly to an advantage to the Bar and its related women. The history of the Abady Trophy, an elegant Victorian silver cup supported by a classical figure, is however more obscure. It was allocated to the match after resting, unnoticed, among the Lincoln's Inn silver, for many years. It was thought to have been presented originally by a Mr Abady, who may have been the husband of Mrs Jacques Abady, an early figure in the Ladies' Legal GA. Ellie Evans organises the solicitors' side of the match.

Chartered Surveyors

The Society has played against the Chartered Surveyors GS since their formation in 1907 when they took pride in the number of Chestertons in their team, one of whom won the French Amateur Championship. Like the Bar and the Ladies' Legal, this fixture was quickly started again after the wars. In the 1950s the game was played at Walton Heath and was particularly popular. Bobby Furber ran the fixture for many years until 1989 when James Furber took over and during this time Martin Christmas, a Walker Cup player, sometimes played for the Surveyors. In recent years the fixture has been organised by Mark Clark and has usually been played at West Sussex, one of the best courses south of London.

Irish Solicitors

It is appropriate that the Society's first regular overseas fixture should begin on the great links courses of Ireland. Arfon Jones organised and led the Society's 12 man team on the expedition in 2006. His counterpart, Henry Lappin, appeared to have undreamed of powers over the Irish team, even, it was rumoured, direct debit arrangements for expenses.

On the first morning in a stiff breeze at County Louth (Baltray) the Irish quickly revealed their competitiveness and established a lead they never surrendered, although the Society made some inroads the next day at The Island to reduce the margin of the final loss to 10 matches to 8. The hospitality was at its Irish best and there was there was never any doubt that this would become a permanent fixture. The next year the Society was on home ground at Brancaster and Hunstanton and playing foursomes. But the Irish were fresh from being crowned champions of lawyers' golf, having conquered legal golfing teams from

Peter Hewes shows resolution as he approaches his putt to halve the entire match against the Irish Solicitors' Golfing Society at Rosses Point in 2008. The body language of the onlookers reveals less confidence: Arfon Jones (in blue shirt) is looking towards the bar and Keith Gallon is reviewing the imminent collapse of the Irish property boom

all over the continent and Ontario and were confident of continuing success. The pre-match sweepstake pointed to another Irish win but the final result was better than anybody had dared predict; a 13 ½ to 4 ½ win for the Society.

In 2008, in WB Yeats's country under Ben Bulben's bare head, at County Sligo (Rosses Point) the whole fixture turned on the players in the final match who were all square playing the short par 4 18th. Peter Hewes and Robin Holmes for the Society and Paddy Donaghy and Michael Quinn for the Irish were told the score after they had each hit good tee shots. Inevitably, the green was not troubled by the second shots but finally Peter Hewes holed a gritty five footer to halve both his own and the overall match. At Saunton in 2009, Henry Lappin produced his strongest side and the Irish had already established an unbeatable lead after two of the three rounds.

Lloyd's

Lloyd's Golf Club was founded in 1894 and is probably the senior English professional body golfing association. The Society played matches against Lloyd's before the First War, although the only known result was a loss in 1907, and Lord Riddell spoke at the Lloyd's Golf Club dinner in 1920. The fixture was revived in July 1953 as a result of a friendship between two Worplesdon members, the Society's Don (Horsey) Kerr and Pat Milligan, that year's captain of Lloyd's. The match has been played every year since; at Worplesdon until 1961, then at the Berkshire until 1988 and since 1989 at New Zealand. The connection was reinforced by Francis Perkins who was a member of both societies after he left Clifford-Turner for insurance.

Beware photographs from the Press. This was produced to mark the mutual centenary of both societies. James Furber, Arfon Jones, Brian Gegg, Mark Clark, Chris Millerchip, Andrew Dixon, Barrie Lloyd and Adam Walker apparently stand proudly behind Lord Riddell. The original was taken at Walton Heath in 1931, just a few months after Riddell had entertained 130 LSGS members to golf, lunch, dinner and all drinks. A close inspection reveals that the two Farrers' partners, James Furber and Adam Walker, were old fashioned enough to look entirely right in their normal golfing kit

Ray Gardner ran the Society's team for many years while the Lloyd's team was run by his son Richard until Richard's death in 1988. After Ray Gardner's death in 1993 part of his legacy to the Society was applied in the purchase of the Ray Gardner Bowl which has been contested by the two teams since 1994. Philip Langford has been the Society's match manager in recent years.

Press

The Press Golfing Society was founded in 1904, the same year as the Society, and matches have been played since 1905, usually at Walton Heath in the early days. Some of these games were ferociously contested with the newspaper proprietors such as George Riddell, Emsley Carr and Frank Newnes, who were themselves good players, fielding ace champions including Harold Hilton and Bernard Darwin at the top of the team. As recorded in the first chapter, the Society reciprocated by getting out its best players.

Riddell, that extraordinary accumulator of positions, titles and influence, was actively involved in both societies and was Captain of the London Press (as it then was) in 1907 and President from 1920 to 1934, as well as Captain of LSGS in 1910 and President from 1911 to 1914 and then again from 1926 to 1934. He normally played for the Press but stepped aside in his year of captaincy of the London Solicitors GS, only to come back the next year and win both his matches to help the Press inflict a rare defeat on LSGS. Judging by the Press's centenary book, he was equally generous to the members of both societies, although LSGS was never entertained at the Savoy, a venue reserved for the press barons and their scribes.

There was much rivalry between the press proprietors and Lord Northcliffe of *The Times* was jealous of Riddell's influence at Walton Heath and the London

The London Solicitors' Golfing Society

Press and, although he became a member of the Press society in 1911, he started his own golfing society in 1910.

Between the wars the matches were less well recorded and apparently less competitive. After the Second War, the match was in abeyance until revived for the centenary of both societies in 2004. James Furber led the team in the centenary match at Royal St George's, and every year since then, where the course easily outstrips the quality of the golf. The presence of Vyvyan Harmsworth, the Press's president, in the match is a reminder of the great press dynasties.

Stock Exchange

The Stock Exchange was another golfing association with a formidable reputation before the First World War. It was founded in 1905 as the London Stock Exchange Golfing Society and the London Solicitors' GS has been playing the match since at least 1907. Their crack player in the early days was Mure Fergusson, an intimidating looking golfer, who was twice finalist in the Amateur and a dominating figure at Royal St George's where his cartoon, simply entitled "Mure", still guards the entrance to the changing rooms. One young man, perhaps a solicitor in one of the matches, made the mistake of calling him Mure as they were walking to the first tee. He thundered back: "The name, to you sir, is Fergusson and after 12.45 I will not know you".

LSGS has been playing matches at Sandwich for more than a century. In 1914 the 6th (Maiden) hole was still blind but had just been changed from a shot directly over the highest part of the hill. The bunker on the left of the green had not yet been cut. The view towards the 7th hole shows more loose sand than has been seen in recent years

All of the professions with golfing associations have changed greatly since the First World War and none more so than the Stock Exchange where, since its demutualisation at the beginning of the 21st century, there is no direct connection between the Stock Exchange and its member firms. Keith Gallon organised the match at Woking for more than 30 years, with Andrew Dixon taking over in 2010. Gallon's predecessor as match manager, Leslie Nathanson, had continued his practice at LSGS meetings of having Carpenter, his chauffeur, deliver the port to Woking the day before a match to ensure that it would be drinking well.

The Wine Trade

The Wine Trade match is a relatively young fixture by the standards of the London Solicitors' GS even though it was in 1953 that the Captain, Cyril Davenport, reported that he was organising a game. For more than 20 years the match has been organised by Michael Stanford-Tuck, Captain of the Society in 2010, and Edward Demery, until recently managing director of Justerini & Brooks. The match is now played at Royal St George's whose suitably wide and reasonably priced wine list aids the main enjoyment of the day at lunch and, unsurprisingly, is popular with Society members. Indeed, until the last few years, to have any chance of winning, the Society had to be well ahead after the morning round: this was important as the losers were expected to pay for the substantial lunchtime wine bill.

But the cost was reduced by the generosity, for many years, of Edward Demery and Justerini & Brooks in providing vintage port at the lunch. The port was decanted in secret so that a sweepstake could be held to guess the vintage and the shipper. If the vintage was guessed, 50% of the sweepstake money was won (the rest going to charity) and a rare correct answer of vintage and shipper would also win a bottle of the port itself. Edward Demery would go through the answers one by one, eliminating the wildest first. On one occasion Demery's generosity was abused as his glass of Taylor's 1977 was swapped with a lesser port as he was making ex cathedra statements on the quality of the vintage.

CHAPTER ELEVEN

The Match against the Writers to the Signet Golf Club

Peter Morley-Jacob and Stephen Barnard

T HE FIRST MATCH against the Writers to the Signet Golf Club at Sandwich in 1961, fittingly also one of the great years for Bordeaux, has already been described by Bobby Furber. The successful format of four-somes matches on one day followed by a black tie dinner and dinner matches, mixing the two teams, has continued ever since. In 1962 Bobby Furber organised a dinner in the Gondoliers Room at the Savoy to thank Leslie Nathanson for his great lunch the previous year at the Coq d'Or, and the English team then went straight to the station and took the overnight sleeper north. There was breakfast in the North British Hotel, above Waverley Station in Edinburgh, before transferring to the Marine Hotel at North Berwick. The privilege of stay-ing at Greywalls, hard by Muirfield, whose stylish Lutyens buildings are com-plemented by Gertrude Jekyll gardens, came later.

Muirfield has the excellent practice of using six front tees, six middle and six back for everyday golf. For those fortunate enough to have a room at Greywalls facing the course, an early assessment can be made at dawn on Thursday morn-ing of the chances of making the carry at the 10th, particularly if the back tee is in use, and whether it would be better to volunteer to drive at the 1st.

In 1962 Muirfield was established as one of the world's great courses but this was not always the case. Even though he had won the Open on its first playing there in 1892, Harold Hilton complained about the thistles and the roughness of the ground near the greens and "I cannot say that I am at all in love with Muirfield as a test of the game". Later he said "the course at Muirfield, for many reasons, could not be considered a truly severe test of the game, as in addition to its extreme shortness there was far too much of the drive and pitch variety of

Bobby Furber (left), George Cockburn and Tommy Walmsley at Greywalls in 1964 in a rare post-war photograph not taken by Walmsley

(above left) The bar of the Bell Hotel, Sandwich, in 1967. Standing (from left) Alastair Blair, Logan McClure and Roger Inglis and, sitting, Ewen Cameron, John Wilson and Maxwell Ferguson

(above right) The 1978 captains and secretaries discuss pairings: (from left) John Goble, Hugh Allan, Charles Fraser and Peter Morley-Jacob

hole". All this has now changed for the better and LSGS members should take pride in reminding the WS team that it took an English solicitor, Harry Colt, to do so. The course now has some of the best short holes in the world; all played to the Harry Colt speciality of greens perched on the top of sand dunes or hummocks. Colt was wise enough not to touch the 9th hole.

Even then the WS team tried to make changes. During Jimmy Dallmeyer's captaincy of the Honourable Company in 1952-53, the 10th green had been pushed back up the hill so that it would be visible from behind the cross bunkers. This change did not last and the green soon reverted to its previous position, where it remains.

In 1962 the WS team was refreshed by some new players who were to become regulars and won by the tight margin of 10 ½ to 9 ½. The newcomers included Peter McClure, George Cockburn, fresh from a 67 that year in a WSGC meeting at Luffness and a win in the R&A's Calcutta Cup with Stewart Lawson a few weeks before, and a young Douglas Moodie. Don (Horsey) Kerr was the LSGS captain in 1962 and gave a sparkling speech.

The victories in the fixture were relatively even for many years with the London Solicitors' GS usually slightly ahead. This has changed in recent times, particularly since the turn of the century, with the Society pulling ahead into a comfortable lead. Indeed, the WSGC had to win at Muirfield in 2008 to prevent the Society winning 10 years in a row.

For many years the fixture was regarded as a semi-private match and not included on the LSGS fixture card until the early 1990s, although the results were reported annually. Leslie Nathanson was not only one of the originators of this fixture but also a prime mover from its start, with Bobby Furber also heavily involved. In 1976 Peter Morley–Jacob began his long spell as match

manager until Bill Richards took it on in 1999. While only the first few were done on the grand scale (the meal at the Coq d'Or could not be repeated every year or the grand crus of Burgundy would have been exhausted) Nathanson was keen that standards should be maintained and that there should be a mixture of characters and of golfing ability, but with a nucleus of good golfers. A newcomer should be someone who would fit in well with those, from both sides, who had played for a number of years. Only very rarely has an outsider been needed to make up the numbers at the last minute. Probably the most distinguished was John Beck who played for the Scots at Sandwich in 1969, a Walker Cup captain who had played in Victor Longstaffe's Moles team that beat the USA, including Bobby Jones, at Woking in 1926.

There is a considerable burden on the home match manager, which has been done in England for the last 35 years by Peter Morley-Jacob and Bill Richards. The administrative arrangements in Scotland, also splendidly done, have been put in place by the more numerous WSGC secretaries including Ramsay Bissett, Charles Fraser, Ewen Cameron, Peter McClure and Hugh Allan and, later, James Crerar, Ian Boyd, George Russell, Nigel Watt, John Hendry, Alasdair Loudon, Andrew Biggart and Robin MacPherson, with Rab Forman taking over as match manager in 2010.

Leslie Nathanson's Sir Hugh Watson Trophy continues to stand as the physical symbol of the fixture. Later the Writers to the Signet Golf Club presented a Captain's Putter to the Society, believed to be by Hugh Philp, the master clubmaker who died in 1856, which now bears the names of subsequent LSGS captains and is taken to the match each year and, like a parliamentary mace, placed at the head of the table during dinner. In turn, the Society in 1975 gave the WSGC the Donald Kerr putter. The WSGC also presented a quaich for the Soci-

(above left) Roger Davies slumped in his chair as Wales lose to Westen Samoa in the Rugby World Cup in 1991

(above right) Peter Younie and Dick Normand had a different approach to lunch and it was risky to pair them in the afternoon in 1994. This tee shot by Younie at the 6th at Muirfield did not improve matters

ety's centenary.

But the most memorable legacy of the early matches is the great green leather bound volume presented by Tommy Walmsley's widow to the WSGC and containing his excellent photographs. The album is bulky and is stored at the Signet Library in Edinburgh and, like a saint's relics, is taken out only occasionally when the fixture is in Scotland, to be pored over and the comparative ageing of the participants, shown by the photographs, assessed. In more recent years Jonathan Chalton has taken over as the Society's official photographer and a selection of photographs of the match is added each year to the records maintained by the WSGC.

There have been changes over the years. One of the first was caused by the demolition of the Guilford Hotel which prompted a move to the Bell Hotel in Sandwich itself. There has been a steady, if glacial, improvement at the Bell since the 1980s, perhaps funded entirely from the bar profits of the fixture. Indeed the manager once said the match participants were his second best customers. Seeing that LSGS members were somewhat put out, he gave the assurance that in first place were the unassailable Irish Medical Golfing Society. In Scotland the choice of Greywalls has been almost as constant. There was one exception when, on grounds of expense, (Leslie Nathanson would have been horrified) the team returned to the Marine Hotel in North Berwick.

In the early matches, the participants travelled by train, most using the night sleeper: few slept well on the outward journey, but most slept very well on the return. On one trip in the early 1970s, the sleeper car supervisor was particularly attentive to Bill Farrer, apparently confusing him with Richard Marsh, then chairman of British Rail. Travel after the early years has been mainly by air; but even then Leslie Nathanson's generosity could not be restrained when he brought on board champagne and offered it to all the passengers on an otherwise dry flight. The tedium of modern air travel is seeing a return to the train. In either case, the lift to the venue by a host team member has been constant: in the case of Sandwich in the early days using the same road driven by James Bond in his Bentley in *Moonraker*, although on that occasion not to St Mark's, a very thinly disguised Royal St George's.

In common with golf clubs generally, the betting on the dinner matches has in recent years been for token amounts. In the early days the wagers were larger, and the early ones officially recorded in the style of the Honourable Company.

Eating and drinking have however been unchangingly important: for all the competitive banter, this is fundamentally a social event. The teams have dined formally after each match, usually with speeches from both of the Captains, and with invitations to the Captain and Secretary of the host club. In the earlier years this was usually at a hotel, but more recently the Society has enjoyed the grandeur of the dining rooms of Royal St George's and Muirfield.

Richard Grandison stands proudly by the replica of the Maiden green at Sandwich after his hole in one in 1995. Peter Morley-Jacob also had a hole in one in the 1992 match at the 4th at Muirfield. Rumours that any WSGC hole in one has been kept quiet by a parsimonious Scot are unfounded

The speeches have been variable, but usually excellent. Some have been in verse such as Douglas Moodie's Wordsworthian daffodils in 1985. Ronnie Will's poem, "The DKS [Deputy Keeper of the Signet] who plays no golf" contained an alarming image and rhyme when describing the LSGS players:

"Walmsley, massive frame a-wobble,

Nathanson, Gardner and Gob[b]le"

In 1996, Richard Grandison, that year's Society Captain was referring to his school, Fettes, when Guy Robertson-Durham's photograph fell off the wall of the Muirfield dining room. We will never know whether this was coincidence, harmless irritation behind his frame by the Loretto educated Robertson-Durham or perhaps a premonition of the future actions over Iraq of the most famous old Fettesian, Tony Blair.

It took a little time for the current format, now unchanged for many years, to emerge; 20 a side with the match on a Thursday and dinner matches the next day. Once the move had been made to a mid-week fixture a combined team of Writers and Solicitors often played a match locally on the Saturday morning. In the South there was, for many years, a dinner at Royal Cinque Ports on Friday followed by a match against the club the following morning.

Similarly, in Scotland from 1966, a black tie dinner took place at the R&A on Friday evening followed by a match, usually on the Old Course, against the R&A

The facial expressions reflect a narrow win for the Scots in 1997 as Julian Walton (left) hands the Sir Hugh Watson Trophy to Spencer Patrick under the magnificent portrait of Laidlaw Purves, the founder of Royal St George's

on Saturday. Stewart Lawson, a captain and later a trustee of the R&A, often delivered a "witty ditty" at these dinners and became a firm friend of the Society, speaking at Society dinners in London and was later made an honorary member of the Society. Michael Bonallack, five times Amateur Champion and then secretary of the R&A, played in one of the matches, perhaps the best player after Harold Hilton to have played against the Society. Although then past his best, he did hit a two iron through the wind to the 11th green of the Old Course, one of the most dangerous shots in golf, as a reminder of past glory.

On one Saturday morning the view from the Rusacks Hotel overlooking the 18th was of the Old Course, hard as iron under a deep frost. The match was transferred to Elie with its periscope by the first tee and, importantly, sun drenched south facing slopes falling away to the sea.

The R&A matches came to an end with the introduction of the Dunhill tournament which meant the Old Course was no longer available. Even after these original Saturday fixtures had finished, there has always been the opportunity to play golf on Saturday, including fixtures at Bruntsfield and Panmure, where the teams were twice entertained to dinner in the clubhouse, a match against Worlington, and visits to Hankley Common (through Martyn Gowar), Royal Wimbledon, Ashridge and Woking.

Over the years friendships have been built in a way that cannot happen in a one day match. Many members have gone to dinners and rugby matches as the guest of an opposite number. A dinner in the Signet Library, one of the grandest rooms in Europe, is always a splendid sight. On the steps up to the great room, the portraits of Sir Hugh Watson, Pat Oliphant, Ronnie Will and Peter Millar can be admired; all Deputy Keepers of the Signet who have played in the match or spoken at a dinner. After one dinner in London, George Russell, fitter than the average Scot, went straight off to New York to run a marathon and later retired from the law to drive a ski bus in Aspen in Colorado.

Over the years some members of the teams began to travel a day or so early. By the 1970s it was normal for Maxwell Ferguson, Peter Millar and Ewen Cameron to be playing with John Wilson before the Sandwich fixture. Recently, Jonathan Chalton has organised Tuesday games at Rye and Spencer Patrick has done the same at Prestwick. On Tuesday evenings the art could be admired at George Tait's house in Edinburgh. On Wednesday mornings in Scotland there have been games of mixed foursomes at Gullane, originally organised by Sylvia Boyd, the daughter of Logan McClure, with strong female golfers including Barbara McIntosh, former English Ladies Champion. The inadequacies of the visitors' game would be compensated by the first glimpse of Muirfield from the 7th tee of Gullane No 1.

While all this golf was on offer, it was always understood that an acceptance

to play in the fixture involved a commitment to play all day on Thursday and on Friday morning. Most people were however ready for action by lunch on Wednesday, considered by some to be the best moment of the fixture when old friends are met again. For many of the new recruits, initially overawed by the din, there was the prospect of playing one of the world's great courses, perhaps for the first time.

Alasdair Louden tees off at Muirfield with the Firth of Forth in the background. Nigel Bennett admires the ball's progress

And some of the sights for the new recruit could be unusual, alarming even. Peter Younie, who claimed to be the best putter in East Lothian and used his putter from 60 yards, would roar like a sealion in the evenings before finding a comfortable chair in which to close his eyes. He would then, in his sleep, tell all passing by to get out of his bedroom.

David Birrell was another big man, who helped to "put a kilt on" (as he him-self described it) the law relating to the development of the North Sea oil and gas fields. Dick Normand was almost certainly the fiercest competitor on either side, for many years capable of playing to his age, with these attributes evident in his portrait in the Scottish National Portrait Gallery which was presented by Sir Charles Fraser.

All participants will have their own memories of individual matches and the evenings spent at the dinners and in the bars at the Bell and Greywalls; Ray Gardner's air shot on the 13th green at Muirfield; Bobby Furber and Jimmy Lyon at the piano; the fiercely contested bridge matches with Dick Normand,

Looking down the 12th fairway at Muirfield in 2004, with Gullane in the background. Keith Gallon (with hat) has just hit and Hugo Allan has decided to play an iron

Anthony Surtees, Jonathan Chalton and George Russell (in the very early days everybody seemed to play); the contrast between Alastair Campbell's explosions of laughter and Keith Oliver's deep gravel tones. The English would listen graciously as once again Rob Flockhart, Robin Lind, Andy Birrell and David Anderson bemoaned the latest depths reached by Scottish rugby and would agree that Italy had indeed been lucky to win. But both sides were delighted when Wales lost to Western Samoa in the Rugby World Cup, with Roger Davies slumped in front of the television. Several players may have slept in the bath after a dinner, but Julian Walton was brave enough to admit it. On an early occasion Tommy Walmsley had somehow forgotten his dress trousers and, being a man of substance who could not easily borrow from another, the only alternative was his golfing plus fours. Luckily, someone discovered a train that meandered across the country from Woking to Edinburgh and the trousers arrived in time.

There is also a club of those who, having been three up and four to play, managed to lose their match. The inaugural members were Richard Grandison and Steven Turnbull but they have been joined by the drolly amusing Denbeigh Kirkpatrick and Gordon Murray and no doubt others. Foursomes golf can throw up extraordinary results. In 2008, a dinner match at Muirfield was lost even after the losers had won 7 holes in a row and had also halved the 3rd and the 5th in four. The climax was reached on the 17th where Harry Colt's cross bunkers

The teams after the dinner at Muirfield in 2004

ensured one side played 5 shots in a row and the other then played 6 without losing their turn.

The matches remain competitive but in a friendly spirit and the Stewart Lawson description of the WSGC members is not quite right, if indeed it ever was:

"They are full of warmth and bonhomie: I'll say it till I'm hoarse,

That you couldn't meet a nicer bunch of fellows – off the course."

CHAPTER TWELVE

The East Anglian Match
and Aldeburgh

"**B**ETTER PLAY ANOTHER", is the cry at Aldeburgh Golf Club.
There are not many courses where it is possible to lose your ball in
the gorse on every shot on every hole, although this is now more difficult
following some recent gorse clearance. The hazards of foursomes golf at
Aldeburgh are however tempered by the prospect of a pint of Adnams afterwards, in the sunshine on the terrace overlooking the 9th green.

The fixture against the East Anglian lawyers developed from a day of foursomes golf at Aldeburgh in the mid 1970s organised by the Society's John Wilson and Geoffrey Barnard, senior partner of Birketts, the Ipswich based firm,
which Wilson was later to join as a partner.

In 1977, one of the earliest matches, and the first with eight a side, set the
tone and fixed many of the participants, most of whom appeared on a regular
basis. The pairings for the morning's play were:

*Philip Langford (left), Steven
Turnbull, Bill Farrer and Jeremy
Caplan after a match against the
East Anglian solicitors*

Jeremy Caplan & John Wilson v Geoffrey Barnard & Nigel Moore

Bobby Furber & Keith Gallon v Peter Johnson & Tig Staveley-Dick

Bill Farrer & Chris James v Alan Catchpole & Michael Orr

John Goble & Peter Morley-Jacob v Chris Cocksedge & Adrian Halliwell

More than thirty years later seven of these initial players were still participating in the match. The LSGS team was a good blend of senior partners and burgeoning youth (including Jeremy Caplan and Keith Gallon in their impressive youthful prime): all were at some stage Captains of the London Solicitors' Golfing Society. Yet the East Anglians were 3 – 1 ahead at lunch, went on to win, and since then the Society has never been ahead in the series of matches. The edge of the East Anglians is probably due to their determination to win compared to the languid insouciance of the Society, or that is the Society's comforting excuse. In this, the East Anglians were led by the competitive Geoffrey Barnard who won his first eight recorded matches.

David Wybar, the current East Anglian match manager, has produced copious statistics of individual performances which have, in the main, been embargoed from publication to avoid embarrassment. However the percentage of wins on the Society side is particularly impressive from Bruce Streather, Philip Langford, Simon Wilson, Anthony Surtees, Keith Gallon and Steven Turnbull. There are also before and after lunch statistics which should perhaps be permanently deleted, save for noting an 85% win rate in the afternoon for the teetotal and steady Nigel Moore on the East Anglian side.

Aldeburgh Golf Club is a bastion of foursomes golf and the match has usually been rewarded with good weather. It is a rousing sight to come over the crest of a hill on the road into Aldeburgh on a good day and see the white Edwardian clubhouse and the course, gleaming with gorse and broom. Bernard Darwin in an essay on rough said "To summon up the image of a double menace of whins on either side is for me, and I am sure for many other people besides, to think nostalgically of delightful Aldeburgh".

The Aldeburgh smoke room in 1950. The door to the left has been blocked up and the moose's head eventually disintegrated to be replaced by a tiger's head

In the early years, there were parties for the players after the match and on a couple of occasions the London Solicitors' GS has partially repaid the hospitality by hosting dinners at the Wentworth Hotel. At the first dinner the starter was fresh locally grown asparagus. Ever since, the match lunch has started with asparagus from the Suffolk sandlings; and each year several members of the Society collect a bunch of asparagus from Henry Baldry's farm behind the fifth green to impress their spouses with their thoughtfulness.

A match against the East Anglian lawyers in the 1990s. Standing, from left, Richard Grandison, East Anglian player, Giles Webster, Chris Millerchip, Peter Darley, Roger Davies, Adrian Halliwell, Keith Gallon (behind), Jeremy Caplan, Philip Langford, Crow Goodley and Stephen Barnard. Sitting, from left, Chris Cocksedge, Dick Griffiths, Jonathan Chalton, Anthony Surtees, Peter Good, Alan Catchpole and Peter Morley-Jacob. Front, Richard Harris and David Wybar

Regular players on the East Anglian team have included Chris Cocksedge (who was the second match manager), Alan Catchpole, Peter Good, David Wybar, Andrew Gibb, Adrian Halliwell, David Sisson, Chris Schwer and Jeremy Westcott. Indeed Alan Catchpole made 31 consecutive appearances until 2008, apparently getting longer off the tee with each passing year. Twice runner up in the Suffolk Amateur, he was also the last man to pay for his articles at Macfarlanes, claiming to have refused a salary in his second year for fear of losing his amateur status. Iain Pattinson, the lugubrious R&A rules expert seen every year on television for the Open, also plays for East Anglia.

The Society's regulars have included Keith Gallon, Jeremy Caplan, Peter Morley-Jacob (who took over as match manager from John Wilson), Stephen Barnard (the current match manager), Jonathan Chalton, Philip Langford, Anthony Surtees and Harry Anderson. Logan Mair of Ashursts has played for the Society in recent years and in 2009 he almost joined Jeremy Caplan and Bruce Streather as a winner of the President's Putter at Rye. In the final, Jonathan Chalton in searching for Mair's ball on the 16th trod it so deeply into the rough that Mair had to take a drop. *The Times* unkindly commented at the time that even his mother would struggle to love Mair's swing.

There has always been considerable banter (otherwise known as eager anticipation) before and during each match, sometimes even moving to a distinct verbal enthusiasm. On one occasion, Jeremy Caplan phoned Geoffrey Barnard from John Wilson's house very late on the night before the match and got him out of bed, demanding to know the East Anglian pairings. Foolishly, Barnard agreed and, as was to be expected, the details of the LSGS pairings were not provided in return (probably because they did not then exist). Whether such information did anybody any good is doubtful.

Some of the behaviour has been erratic, sometimes even dangerous. In 1997 Adrian Halliwell, a charming man but always unreliable with a club in his hands, was involved in a violent incident. Halliwell's partner, Chris Cocksedge, had driven into a bush on the 10th, their first hole, and Howard Gill, appearing in his first match for the Society, was prodding the bush dutifully with his

Giles Webster, Andrew Gibb, Jeremy Westcott and Stephen Barnard at Aldeburgh in 2009

foot. Halliwell, a man well experienced with gorse, was adopting a more robust approach to the bush but unfortunately only succeeded in bringing the club straight down on top of Gill's foot, bringing a very abrupt and painful end to his day. Worse, Halliwell had used a 7 iron from Howard Gill's own bag of clubs none of which had been put to proper purpose as Gill had yet to play a shot. Despite this, he is given a 0% record in David Wybar's remorseless records: his partner, Richard Matthews, losing the match on his own, perhaps fearful of what might happen next.

On another occasion Bobby Furber, at the time a member of the Rules Committee of the R&A, questioned the legality (and indeed the advisability, in view of the danger) of having to play the ball where it lay hard against the sleepers forming the face of the bunker at the 4th hole. Under the Rules the ball could be lifted and dropped, in the absence of a local rule making the sleepers an integral part of the course. These expert observations on the rules were reported to the Aldeburgh Committee, who promptly made just such a local rule to maintain the existing practice of playing the ball as it lay.

Unknown to the participants in the early matches, other than Bobby Furber, were the Society's much earlier connections with Aldeburgh. In 1904, when the London Solicitors' Golfing Society was founded, Aldeburgh was already 20 years old and many LSGS members, with second houses on the Suffolk coast, were members. Thomas Fenwick, the first Secretary of the Society, was a member and Captain of Aldeburgh in 1910; suffering every captain's worst nightmare when the clubhouse burnt down a few weeks after he took office. His partner, Ernest Longstaffe, had already been captain of Aldeburgh in 1900 and was Captain of the Society in 1909.

His son, Victor Longstaffe, was a member of the Society and is known to

Victor Longstaffe in 1910

every Aldeburgh member, past and present, having been captain twice in 1925 and 1934 and President from 1948 to 1968. He was also captain of golf at Cambridge in 1908 and co-founder of the Moles in 1911 (two other Aldeburgh members were also co-founders). Bernard Darwin commented in 1910 that "he has an extremely neat and attractive style, and is especially to be feared in the neighbourhood of the green". Victor Longstaffe was the runner up in the Worplesdon mixed foursomes in 1929, many years before Jeremy Caplan's three wins in that event, playing with Joy Winn, another Aldeburgh member and an English international. Joy Winn was a friend of Bernard Darwin, one of the Society's most formidable early opponents and an honorary member of Aldeburgh, and she saw Darwin hit his last golf shot, a four iron to the ninth green at Aldeburgh.

Sam Garrett, a founding member of both LSGS and Aldeburgh, was later President of the Law Society. He was also the first solicitor to take a female articled clerk, influenced no doubt by his older sisters Elisabeth Garrett Anderson and Millicent Fawcett. Elizabeth Garrett Anderson, the wife of J G S Anderson, the driving force and first Captain of Aldeburgh, was the country's first female doctor and the first female mayor. She ensured that women have always had equal rights at Aldeburgh, although her handicap of 50 indicates a lack of interest in golf. Millicent Fawcett was President of National Union of Women's Suffrage Societies.

A London solicitor, albeit not a Society member, also held the Aldeburgh record for the course before it was altered in 2008. In 1984, in the special medal to mark the centenary of the club, John Lloyd managed to go round the course in 65, finishing with a nerveless three at the 18th, breaking the course record of 68 by three shots and becoming the first person, amateur or professional, ever to better Aldeburgh's brutal par of 68 in a medal.

CHAPTER THIRTEEN

Golfing Law Firms and the Stoneham Porringer

I N T H E E A R L Y D A Y S of the London Solicitors' Golfing Society the idea of the golfing law firm and competition between law firms did not exist. The most important early firm was the small partnership of Dod, Longstaffe and Fenwick of 16 Berners Street, W1 where Thomas Fenwick, the first Secretary, and Ernest Longstaffe, an early Captain, were partners and where Victor Longstaffe was an articled clerk.

In the inter-war years there are echoes of law firms in the names of newly admitted members, such as Joynson-Hicks, Theodore Goddard and Oswald Hickson, although some of these firms have now merged or the name otherwise lost.

It was only after the Second War that this changed. Gordon Petch was a member of the City of London Solicitors' Company and had won the Company's cup in 1937. It was in 1948 and 1949, which included Petch's year as Captain, that a successful recruiting of new members, particularly among the City firms and the members of the Solicitors' Company, was undertaken. Also, a new competition,

The pond at the 16th at Woking catches the sunlight during a centenary match

Slaughter and May have been strong supporters of LSGS. Richard Grandison (left), Peter Morley-Jacob and Ian Goldie at Slaughter and May's offices for the dinner before the centenary game with the Bar GS

the Stoneham Porringer, had recently been introduced for the best foursomes score by members of the same firm which quickly became one of the most coveted prizes.

Gordon Petch's firm, Markby, Stewart & Wadesons, and its various predecessors and successors in a family tree possibly even more complicated than that of Fairport Convention, have probably the longest connection with the London Solicitors' GS. Thomas Markby, a relative of the Henry Markby known to Oscar Wilde, had presented silver candlesticks as a prize in 1909 and Robert Nesbitt was President in the 1920s, although it is to be hoped that he is the only officer to have re-joined after being expelled for non-payment of his subscription. Gordon Petch and LC Bullock won the Stoneham Porringer in the first three years from 1947-49 and the firm, currently incarnated as CMS Cameron McKenna, have won a total of 9 times with Arfon Jones and Peter Hewes, with 6 wins, being particularly successful at the turn of the century.

Slaughter and May have been great supporters of the Society, particularly in the mid post war period, with Peter Marriage and Tommy Walmsley (with their photographs) and a little later Peter Morley-Jacob (with his administrative skills), Clive Rumbelow, Martin Read, Richard Grandison and Ian Goldie. The firm boasts 6 Stoneham Porringer wins. In the 1920s, an articled clerk at Slaughter and May, T A (Dale) Bourn, received calls from Buckingham Palace about golf with Edward, Prince of Wales and, a little later, was English Amateur champion at Burnham.

Lovell White and King (later Lovells and now Hogan Lovells) were particularly prominent in the immediate post war period, with a supportive senior partner in Ben Hutchings and three Secretaries of LSGS in Tony Nieland, Jack Hutchings and Gordon Toland, and have won the Stoneham Porringer 6 times.

Clifford-Turner (later Clifford Chance) were also great supporters of the Society in the post-war years with Bobby Furber (Secretary, Captain and President), Raymond Clifford-Turner, Francis Perkins and John Parry-Jones and, later, Robin Burleigh but have only managed 2 Stoneham Porringer wins.

Farrer & Co have, in recent years, been probably the strongest supporters of the London Solicitors' GS with two Secretaries, James Furber and Adam Walker, and a little earlier Bill Farrer and Dick Griffiths as prominent members. The support has however only yielded two Stoneham Porringer victories. Since Farrer & Co's 2001 merger with Crocker & Co, the firm can also claim a connection with Sir William Crocker who presented the Crocker Trophy.

Linklaters' Society members include Chris James, Steven Turnbull, Brinsley

Nicholson and Christopher Johnson-Gilbert and they have won the Porringer four times.

The players from Norton Rose, Giles Botterell, Anthony Surtees and Jonathan Chalton, have been more successful with 6 Stoneham Porringer victories. Surtees and Chalton have proved a particularly potent partnership on the golf course and also at the bridge table, with their chat being very much part of both games.

Adrian Watney with 8 wins for Masons, shared equally with his father, Jack, and Barrie Lloyd, has been the most successful individual player in the Stoneham Porringer. On one occasion, the Watney family failed to defend their title by turning up a day late to the meeting.

Herbert Smith, despite the efforts of David Higginson, John Goble, Hedley Maxwell Wood, Stephen Barnard, Harry Anderson and Andrew Brown, have only managed a single win.

Jonathan Chalton (left) at Sandwich in 1999 talking to Barrie Lloyd. They are multiple Stoneham Porringer winners with their respective partners Anthony Surtees and Adrian Watney

Allen & Overy (with two Stoneham Porringer victories) have for many years, in the Society, been synonymous with Roger Davies and John Rink. Roger Davies is a player good enough to have won the scratch prize in the Senior Golfers' Society's Championship in 2008, following his LSGS predecessors Herbert Taylor and Jeremy Caplan. The ebullient John Rink, as Allen & Overy's managing partner, led the international expansion of the firm.

Nabarro Nathanson hold the record for the three Porringer victories by name partners, Leslie Nathanson and Felix Nabarro, and Leslie Nathanson is the presenter of the most trophies to the Society.

Martyn Gowar and Bill Richards were successive senior partners of Lawrence Graham and are prominent members of the Society. The firm also boasts Henry Johnson, another former senior partner and one of the firm's few remaining annuitants, who is one of the oldest surviving LSGS members joining in 1936. A surfeit of senior partners has however failed to secure a Stoneham Porringer win for Lawrence Graham. Gordon Dadds have had Ray Gardner, Michael Tussaud, Hugh Elder and David Ruck as partners and they finally won the Stoneham Porringer in 2007, albeit with the very low score of 25 points and rumours that they might have been the only competitors. In the early years, the golfing skills of Bob McGill helped to secure two Porringer wins for E F Turner, later to become part of Turner Kenneth Brown (later still absorbed into Nabarro Nathanson).

Travers Smith have Andrew Barrow and Sam Elworthy, both good players.

Andrew Barrow's bald dome can always be seen at LSGS meetings and matches, gleaming in the distance like the Taj Mahal, as he recounts another story with a wry smile on his lips. In recent years Kennedys, led by Matt Andrews, have won several team events including the Centenary under-40 team competition.

Importantly, some of the major firms have been seeding grounds for the Society in encouraging more junior members who have then joined other firms. Two players, Bobby Furber and Philip Langford, have won the Stoneham Porringer with different firms.

One leading law firm that does not appear to have been much involved in the Society is Freshfields, although Jo Rickard was the first female Committee member. In the early days there were close connections with Walton Heath where four Freshfield family members were original shareholders and Riddell's acquisition of a majority interest in the course was completed at Freshfields' offices. Edwin Freshfield was a director and Steward of the Manor and had to deal with commoners' rights over Walton Heath, which were finally resolved much later, partly on the advice of Brian Meaby, a LSGS member and, like his father Harold, a partner of Meaby & Co.

A look at the 20th century winners of the Stoneham Porringer shows how few of those 17 firms are still practising under the name shown on the trophy; only Slaughter and May, Herbert Smith, Allen & Overy and Farrer & Co. Slaughter and May have also so far not added LLP to their name to take up the potential protection of becoming a limited liability partnership. Until the arrival of email in the late 20th century, in addition to relatively stable names, a solicitor could recognise at a glance a letter from a law firm by its colour, from the subtly different shades of cream of the writing paper of Slaughter and May, Norton

Rose and Allen & Overy to the greys of Clifford-Turner and Herbert Smith, and also by its design and the list of partners

The equivalent firm event at the Spring meeting is the Liberty Bowl where one of the firm representatives must be under the age of 35 to try and encourage the younger players. Unusually, Tom Cowgill and Justin Jagger were both under 35 when they won for Herbert Smith in 1994. In 2005 the upper age limit was increased to 45 as only Lawrence Graham and Farrers were regularly entering a team.

The final mention should go to PLC, not a law firm at all, where Chris Millerchip is a proprietor and was Secretary of the Society and Stuart Murray has in recent years organised the Autumn meeting.

Brian Gegg's finish on the 1st tee at Sandwich looks posed but the tee peg shows he has made contact with the ball

For LSGS members practising in the City and also members of the City of London Solicitors' Company there has been an opportunity to be, in effect, a member of a club within a club. The City Solicitors' Company has had a golf section since at least 1911, the year of the first playing of the City of London Solicitors' Company Cup. The Company however failed to organise a competition for the cup in the late 1920s, and in 1931 the Cup was first played for as part of the Society's meeting, but was only available to be won by members of the Company who were also LSGS members. This arrangement has continued ever since.

The history of the Stoneham Porringer is not so clear cut. Robert Stoneham of Stoneham & Sons presented the Porringer to the City of London Solicitors' Company in 1938 "for inter firm foursomes golf competition". Robert Stoneham joined the Society at the beginning of 1949, almost certainly as a result of Gordon Petch's recruitment drive among the City firms. Later that year special mention was made of the Stoneham Porringer in the notice of the Autumn meeting. Having won it for the third time at the meeting, Petch later specifically asked that the names of the winners should be included in the booklet John Haslam sent to all members at the beginning of 1950. The booklet makes it clear that the City of London Solicitors' Company Cup is only open to members of the Company but nothing is said about any qualification for the Stoneham Porringer. The Porringer has always been played for as a foursomes firm event as Robert Stoneham intended and, in living memory at least, not necessarily limited to members of the Company, although in the early days it was usually won by a City based firm and the team members were probably Company members.

Roger Davies, Jonathan Chalton, Frank Donagh and Anthony Surtees by the first tee at Walton Heath in 1996 - a winning team in the Prince Arthur Cup for the City of London Solicitors' Company

In 1978 the Solicitors' Company checked on its silver, no doubt because of the silver price bubble, (and the Stoneham Porringer was then valued at £2,500) and gave its view that the Porringer should only be available to members of the Company. Perhaps forgetting the 1978 request, the London Solicitors' GS approached the City of London Solicitors' Company again in 1991 for a contribution for a plinth and received a similar response on non-members of the Solicitors' Company competing for the Porringer. This dispute has never been resolved and the Stoneham Porringer continues, as before, to be open to all firms at the Society's Autumn meetings and indeed in 2006 was won by solicitors representing Weil, Gotshal & Manges, an American law firm.

The Solicitors' Company golf teams are, however, in practice invariably made up of LSGS members. The most important event is the Prince Arthur Cup, which is a bogey competition for all the livery companies played each year at Walton Heath, involving as many as 60 teams, and with 240 participants one of the largest amateur events in the country. The Company's four man team has been captained by Anthony Surtees for more than 20 years, and has been successful on several occasions. The cup is one of the biggest, as fits the donor, Prince Arthur, the Duke of Connaught, the last surviving son of Queen Victoria and who had the Duke of Wellington as a godfather. A large vehicle is needed to take it away as Surtees discovered when the cup, and its plinths and box, would not fit into his Mini.

CHAPTER FOURTEEN

The Centenary and Beyond
2004 to 2010

THOMAS FENWICK, Herbert Taylor, Vivian Pollock, Charles Murray Smith and the other signatories of the letter of 16th March 1904 to London solicitors "known to be golfers" would have been proud of the London Solicitors' Golfing Society on its centenary. It had remained true to its original purpose that "an Association or Club for Solicitors and Articled Clerks ..., would be popular among London Solicitors, as the Club could hold Meetings and Competitions amongst its own Members, and play Matches with kindred Associations".

James Furber had been promoted to the Captaincy in 2004 for a specially extended term to oversee the celebrations. The burden of taking over as Secretary in the centenary year fell to Chris Millerchip. The preparations for the centenary had begun as early as 1994 when Jonathan Chalton agreed to begin work on the history of the Society, the writing of which itself became a Homeric tale characterised, in the main, by small steps rather than giant leaps. However, it is good to know that this book has arrived in less time than it took Odysseus to return from the Trojan wars.

The Centenary committee did an excellent job: everything was to the point and Millennium Dome excesses were avoided. The chairman was Philip Langford, who had been Captain in 1994 and has been a consistent supporter of the Society. A big man, he is deceptively long and a determined matchplayer. He received the ultimate compliment from Padraig (Judd) Duffy, himself one of a very competitive Irish side, "Philip, the problem with you is you just don't know how to lose". His devotion to duty is shown by his ripped trousers and grazed leg suffered on the escalators at Kings Cross after a full participation in a centenary committee meeting at Farrer & Co. Philip Langford personally organised the centenary knock out, the first such event for several decades, which was won by Jamie Hudson who beat Andrew Barrow in the final. Jamie Hudson had luck riding with him; not only did he have a hole in one at the first hole at Huntercombe in an earlier round against Robin Burleigh, but the bar was empty when

Philip Langford on the 1st tee at Muirfield in 1998

(left) Jamie Hudson (right), the winner of the centenary match-play knock-out, receives the congratulations of Andrew Barrow, the losing finalist

(right) Lord Griffiths telling his favourite Councillor Williams joke at the Centenary Dinner in 2004

he came in. The centenary knockout was appropriate as the Society's first competition had been a knock out, and between the Wars as many as three a year were completed, each with its own cup.

Barrie Lloyd, almost singlehandedly, organised the centenary dinner at Middle Temple Hall on 25th March 2004, just one day after the centenary, which was subsidised to some extent by Ray Gardner's legacy. A highlight was Hugh Griffiths's tortuous story about Councillor Williams, with numerous elaborations, as his voice became more and more Welsh. As well as being an accomplished after dinner speaker who has spoken at Society dinners over three decades, Lord Griffiths has achieved the unique hat trick of being a senior Law Lord, Captain of the R&A and President of the MCC. But the enduring memento of the evening was an illustrated four page short history of the Society's origins and early days, put together by Bobby Furber and Jonathan Chalton, which was at each place on coming through for dinner.

The previous Autumn the LSGS Challenge had been held at Walton Heath; an inter-firm team event for those under 40. It was won by Matt Andrews and Paul Carter of Kennedys, who played the last nine holes in one under par for 27 points to squeeze past Linklaters. The London Solicitors' GS returned again to Walton Heath, once dominated by Lord Riddell and the scene of so many early matches and meetings, for the Centenary Invitation meeting in September 2004. Robin Holmes, with his guest Allan Chisholm, won the prize, narrowly preventing another success by Matt Andrews.

There was also a centenary foursomes match against Prestwick which LSGS surprisingly won by 5 wins to 2. The match was organised with the help of Spencer Patrick, later President of the Writers to the Signet GC and a Prestwick member, but the Society was too late to have been served by Mr Bennett, the famously miserable Prestwick steward. Perhaps he modelled himself on Lane,

Algernon Moncrieff's's butler, who, on being told by Moncrieff that he was a perfect pessimist, replied: "I do my best to give satisfaction, sir". Adrian Watney once made the mistake of asking Bennett for a Pimms and the response was "We don't serve exotic drinks at Prestwick, sir".

Adam Walker, one of James Furber's partners at Farrers and a powerful striker of the ball who won the scratch medal at the Spring meeting in 1998, had organised the Invitation meeting. He was rewarded by being made Dinner Secretary the next year with a view to becoming Secretary in due course, it having been decided that 5 year terms would be more sensible in the future. For some reason he retained this Prince of Wales type position when he succeeded Chris Millerchip as Secretary and Treasurer in 2008, thus achieving the dubious distinction of holding more elected offices at the same time than any other person in the Society's history. Perhaps, like an actor playing Falstaff, he had so grown into the role that it was a shame to change it.

Chris Millerchip, another powerful man and a big hitter, was from a professional point of view, a different Secretary: the first not to be a partner in a law firm. He is a proprietor of PLC, the providers of legal information, in particular on-line services. PLC has been a valued sponsor of the Society, particularly of events for the younger player, and it was appropriate that Chris Millerchip helped PLC to win the foursomes prize in the LSGS Challenge for the under-40s. During his years as Secretary, from 2003 to 2008 when he moved to the United States, the Society began to use email for notices giving the added anticipation of the notification of tee times by email shortly before a meeting. A domain name had been secured by Nigel Bennett as long ago as 2000, and eventually in 2010 Andrew Brydon arranged for the Society to join the rest of the world with its own website. In all other respects the London Solicitors' Golfing Society remains remarkably similar to the club created by the founders in 1904, who would have recognised most of the courses played by the Society.

The remaining member of the Centenary Committee, other than James Furber, was Bill Richards, then senior partner of Lawrence Graham. He had been Captain in 1992 and since 1999 has been the patient organiser of the Writers' match: he knows that 40 middle aged men in dinner jackets are more diffi-

(top) Many guests from "kindred associations" came to the centenary dinner. Gillie Barratt, organiser of the Ladies' Legal, and David Wybar, organiser of the East Anglian lawyers, flank Peter Gardiner-Hill, a past Captain of the R&A

(bottom) Chris Millerchip, the Secretary, putting at Prestwick in 2004 watched by Julian Walton

cult to get on a bus than the same number of 5 year olds. Perhaps his father, Arthur Richards, had given him some tips as he was for many years the leading light in the Stage GS who had played matches against the Society in the 1920s.

The energy of the centenary year continued in subsequent years with the focus, correctly, on the need for more and younger members. A dinner for the under 45s (relatively young in Society terms) was held in 2005. The quaich presented by the Writers to the Signet Golf Club for the Society's centenary was allocated to the best score by an under 45 player at the Spring meeting and was won for the first time by Jack Riddy. All of this is commendable as, without a substantial boost of younger members, the Society might gradually fade away, particularly as the baby boom generation ages.

The older players were in the meantime continuing to give a good account of themselves. At the Spring meeting in 2009 Bruce Streather won a fifth scratch prize at that meeting with a fine 71, claiming he needed four pars for a 68, 30 years after his first win. He had already showed his golfing longevity in 2001 by becoming the oldest winner of the Oxford and Cambridge GS's President's Putter, having a suitably senior nap in his car over lunch between the semi-final and the final.

Little did anybody realise on that warm May day at Woking, that 2009 was almost to be the year for the ultimate achievement for the older golfer, or perhaps any older sportsman. Tom Watson has most of the attributes needed to be a member of the Society; he is a brisk player, a lover of links golf and the traditions of the game, is conservatively dressed, has proved himself on "well known courses", is reported to like a glass of beer every now and then and, most significantly, is older than the Archbishop of Canterbury. Tom Watson's colossal struggle at Turnberry with the great Jack Nicklaus in the 1977 Open Championship, even more than 30 years before, is remembered by all golfers over 45 as if it was yesterday. And every one of those watched in 2009 as Tom Watson's second shot on the 72nd hole on the same course in the Open, all those years later, was punished more than the quality of the shot deserved as it went just too far and rolled down the hump behind the flag - and they all hoped for the best but feared for the worst.

The Society's second century has seen the match play competition become a permanent fixture, perhaps because it enabled the younger members to play at the weekends, with Philip Langford continuing to chase up the competitors. The second playing was won by Jeremy Caplan and the third by the relatively

youthful Brian Gegg who was Captain in 2007. Langford has also presented a Victorian salver as a trophy for the matchplay.

And it was only two years after the centenary that the first regular overseas fixture began, more than 90 years after Robson Sadler first took a team to Dublin, with a defeat inflicted by the Irish Solicitors at Baltray (County Louth) and The Island. Arfon Jones, Captain in 2001, organised the team and even a heart attack could not prevent him taking revenge the next year at Brancaster and Hunstanton.

2010 not only saw Woking consolidate its position as the most used venue for a Society meeting but LSGS members played on the first new course for a Society meeting in almost 50 years, with the Autumn meeting held at Ashridge. More importantly, it may have been the only time when a Society member, Richard Grandison and Philip Langford respectively, was in each case the Captain of the host club. The use of Ashridge was also the first time since 1973 that a Society meeting had been held north of London; an occasion when Jack and Adrian Watney, clearly disorientated, turned up a day late at Moor Park to defend the Stoneham Porringer they had won for the three preceding three years.

One definition of a good day's golf is two rounds of foursomes where each round takes less time than the lunch. This is increasingly difficult to do as golf is one of few games where the speed of play is directly affected by the pace of people playing in different matches. Foursomes golf is at the core of the Society, and the golf is therefore played on traditional two ball courses, and some members are very happy to go from one year to the next without playing fourball golf. The formal decision by the Committee in 1937 to use foursomes for all competitions has never been abandoned.

(above left) The committee hard at work at its 2010 meeting in the boardroom of Farrer & Co. From left, Mark Clark, Peter Morley-Jacob, James Furber, Jeremy Caplan, Christopher Johnson-Gilbert, Matt Andrews (back to camera), Chris Millerchip (obscured) and Adam Walker

(above right) Adam Walker (left) and Chris Millerchip, the two most recent Secretaries, beside the Society's trophies for the 2010 Spring meeting at Woking. Also on display are socks in LSGS colours as well as the LSGS tie

It is a truism that golden ages are always in the past. The London Solicitors' GS was fortunate to be formed in the golden age of the amateur sportsman, before the First World War ended the wealth and leisure of the Edwardian era. Herbert Taylor, Vivian Pollock and Victor Longstaffe were well known figures whose names regularly appeared in the national and golfing papers. Taylor deserves particular mention as probably the Society's best player; he was a finalist in the 1908 Amateur and his 73 in the second round of the 1911 Open was better than any by Harry Vardon, the winner. The second golden age is linked to the driven figure of Lord Riddell and his hospitality at the Summer meetings at Walton Heath until his death in 1934. The third began in the 1950s, initiated by Gordon Petch and John Haslam and continued by Bobby Furber, Leslie Nathanson, Ray Gardner and others. Fortunately, the modern day members continue to maintain the London Solicitors' Golfing Society's reputation as one of the best golfing societies.

Officers

Presidents

1904–1906 Thomas Rawle
1906–1907 James S Beale
1907–1908 Charles Murray Smith
1908–1911 James S Beale
1911–1914 Sir George Riddell
1914–1921 Sir Ellis Cunliffe
1921–1922 Rt Hon David Lloyd George MP
1922–1924 Sir Joseph Hood Bt MP
1924–1925 Robert C Nesbitt MP
1925–1926 Edmund R Cook
1926–1934 Rt Hon Lord Riddell
1935–1937 Sir Harry Pritchard
1937–1938 Sir Reginald Poole
1938–1953 Sir Thomas Barnes
1953–1964 Sir Dingwall Bateson
1964–1972 F Gordon Petch
1973–1982 Leslie M Nathanson
1982–1990 F R (Bobby) Furber
1990–1993 Raymond F Gardner
1994– Peter J Morley–Jacob

Vice Presidents

1919–1934 Thomas C Fenwick
1921–1927 Sir Ellis Cunliffe
1922–1945 Rt Hon David Lloyd George MP
1922–1926 Rt Hon Lord Riddell
1922–1964 The President of the Law Society for the time being
1930–1932 Viscount Brentford (formerly William Joynson–Hicks)
1935–1939 C V Young
1939–1947 Sir Edmund Cook
1948–1951 Harold Forbes White
1949–1968 G D Hugh–Jones
1952–1965 R E Attenborough
1964–1978 John D Haslam
1969–1982 F R (Bobby) Furber
1978–1980 Tommy P Walmsley

1980–1990 Raymond F Gardner
1982–1984 Jack D Watney
1984–2004 W O (Bill) Farrer
1990–1994 Peter J Morley–Jacob
1994– Jeremy J N Caplan
1994– Jonathan N L Chalton
2005– W James Furber

Captains

1904–1907 Charles Murray Smith
1907 Cyril Plummer
1908 J A C Tanner
1909 Ernest V Longstaffe
1910 Sir George Riddell
1911 James Hall
1912 Henry Mossop
1913 T Litton Taylor
1914–1919 T Rothwell Haslam
1920–1922 C V Young
1922 Harold Forbes White
1923 L W Webster
1924 H Robson Sadler
1925 W M Woodhouse
1926 C E Stredwick
1927 B Trayton Kenward
1928–1930 Sydney Newman
1930 E S Trehearne
1931 R P Hamp
1932 P W Russell
1933 J Arthur Attenborough
1934 Richard O J Dallmeyer
1935 T E St C Daniell
1936 Malcolm Clark
1937 SK Nichols
1938 J L de la Cour
1939–1946 Charles N T Jeffreys
1946–1948 Arnold Carter
1948 G D Hugh–Jones
1949 F Gordon Petch

1950 W L Pengelly
1951 E H Coe
1952 G W Fisher
1953 Cyril Davenport
1954 Francis L Perkins
1955 Ben L B Hutchings
1956 John D Haslam
1957 R H R (Bob)McGill
1958 C J Gordon Woolley
1959 Peter Marriage
1960 Tom M Sowerby
1961 Leslie M Nathanson
1962 J Don (Horsey) Kerr
1963 T Gerald Bennett
1964 John G Gamble
1965 F R (Bobby) Furber
1966 Arthur J R Blok
1967 H Mott
1968 P Mike Armitage
1969 G Pat O'N Pearson
1970 Geoff R E Wallis
1971 W O (Bill) Farrer
1972 Raymond F Gardner
1973 Tommy P Walmsley
1974–1976 Jack D Watney
1976–1978 John A P Wilson
1978–1980 John F Goble
1980 Jeremy J N Caplan
1981 Keith S Gallon
1982 Anthony C Surtees
1983 Frank Donagh
1984 Peter J Morley–Jacob
1985 Robin H Burleigh
1986 J Adrian Watney
1987 Chris R L James
1988 Jonathan N L Chalton
1989 H Clive Rumbelow
1990 Roger G Davies
1991 Barrie O Lloyd
1992 B W D (Bill) Richards
1993 John S Rink
1994 Philip J D Langford
1995 John P Hargrove
1996 Richard N S Grandison
1997 Julian F J Walton
1998 Martyn C Gowar
1999 Stephen G Barnard
2000 Nigel B Bennett
2001 Arfon Jones
2002 Steven M Turnbull
2003–05 W James Furber

2005 Mark C C Clark
2006 Andrew J Barrow
2007 Brian G Gegg
2008 Andrew J Dixon
2009 Peter L Hewes
2010 Michael D Stanford–Tuck

Secretary and Treasurer

1904–1919 Thomas C Fenwick
1904–1910 Herbert E Taylor (Joint Secretary)
1919–1927 B Trayton Kenward (there was no Treasurer 1922–1924)
1927–1948 Harold Forbes White
1948–1956 John D Haslam (ceased to be Treasurer in 1955)

Secretary

1956–1963 F R (Bobby) Furber
1963–1965 A R (Tony) Nieland
1965–1969 G Jack B Hutchings
1969–1974 Gordon K Toland
1974–1987 Peter J Morley–Jacob
1987–2003 W James Furber

Secretary and Treasurer

2003–2008 Chris J Millerchip (became Treasurer in 2006)
2008– Adam D Walker

Treasurer

1955–1969 Cyril Davenport
1969–1979 John G Parry Jones
1979–1985 Chris R L James
1985–2006 Barrie O Lloyd

Fixtures Secretary

1974–1980 Graham Millar
1980–2009 J Adrian Watney
2009– Chris J Millerchip

Dinner Secretary

2005– Adam D Walker

Winners of the Society's trophies

Scratch Gold Medals

In 1913 and 1914, and again from 1927, a Gold Medal was presented to the winner of the scratch medal at the Society's meetings; from 1930 this was only done at the Summer Meeting. Gold Medals were not presented after the Second World War.

1913	Ashford Manor	No record	
1914	Ashford Manor	Robert L. Pillman	
1915–26	No Competition for a Gold Medal		
1927 Summer	Walton Heath	Sydney Newman	84
1927 Autumn	Addington	H. Forbes White	79
1928 Summer	Walton Heath	R.W. Ripley	81
1928 Autumn	R.A.C. Epsom	W.D. Robinson	80
1929 Summer	Walton Heath	R.E. Johnson	
1929 Autumn	R.A.C. Epsom	R.W. Ripley	77
1930 Summer	Walton Heath	L. Evelyn Jones	
1931 Summer	Walton Heath	R.A.P. Fison	76
1932 Summer	Walton Heath	R.W. Ripley	80
1933 Summer	Walton Heath	R.W. Ripley	78
1934 Summer	Walton Heath	C.J.Y. Dallmeyer	75
1935 Summer	Walton Heath	F.R.E. Thairlwall	76
1936 Summer	Addington Palace	R.W. Ripley	
1937 Summer	St George's Hill	E.A.S. Brooks	
1938 Summer	Addington	E.A.S. Brooks	76
1939 Summer	West Hill	E.A.S. Brooks	82

Spring Meeting Scratch Medal
Crocker Trophy

From 1954 the winner of the scratch medal at the Spring Meeting has received the Crocker Trophy which was presented by Sir William Charles Crocker.

1948	Sandy Lodge	F.G. Petch	79
1949	West Hill	D.I.C. Cooke	79
1950	Moor Park	F.L. Perkins	76
1951	Walton Heath	F.R. Hamp	83
1952	Porters Park	H.W. Meaby	72
1953	Berkshire	No record	
1954	Worplesdon	J.D. Kerr	
1955	Addington	J.D. Kerr	78
1956	St George's Hill	H.W. Meaby	

1957	Camberley Heath	D.I.C. Cooke	
1958	New Zealand	J.D. Kerr	
1959	Woking	F.R. Furber	79
1960	Worplesdon	H.W. Meaby	
1961	Woking	J.G. Parry-Jones	
1962	Burhill	J.G. Parry-Jones	
1963	Woking	J.D. Kerr	
1964	Royal Wimbledon	M.A. Blok	
1965	Walton Heath	M.A. Blok	
1966	Berkshire	J.G. Parry-Jones	
1967	Wentworth	F.R. Furber	
1968	Berkshire	R. Burleigh	
1969	Sunningdale	No record	
1970	Berkshire	No record	
1971	Swinley Forest	No record	
1972	Royal Ashdown Forest	No record	
1973	Addington	No record	
1974	Worplesdon	No record	
1975	Wentworth	No record	
1976	New Zealand	K.S. Gallon	
1977	Woking	J.J.N. Caplan	
1978	Woking	S.D. Wilson	
1979	Woking	B.G. Streather	
1980	Woking	J.J.N. Caplan	
1981	Woking	J.J.N. Caplan	
1982	Woking	S.D. Wilson	
1983	Woking	B.G. Streather	
1984	Woking	A.C. Surtees	
1985	Woking	K.S. Gallon	
1986	Woking	J.J.N. Caplan	
1987	Woking	K.S. Gallon	
1988	Woking	B.G. Streather	
1989	Woking	J.J.N. Caplan	
1990	Woking	J.J.N. Caplan	
1991	Woking	J.J.N. Caplan	
1992	Woking	J.J.N. Caplan	
1993	Woking	Justyn Jagger	
1994	Woking	Gordon Simmonds	
1995	Woking	Julian Walton	
1996	Woking	Tom Cowgill	
1997	Woking	Philip Langford	
1998	Woking	Adam Walker	
1999	Woking	Steven Turnbull	
2000	Woking	Steven Turnbull	
2001	Woking	Steven Turnbull	
2002	Woking	Christopher Johnson-Gilbert	
2003	Woking	Philip Langford	76
2004	Woking	Anthony Surtees	78
2005	Woking	Steven Turnbull	75
2006	Woking	Steven Turnbull	74
2007	Woking	Roger Davies	79
2008	Woking	David Ferreira	70
2009	Woking	Bruce Streather	71
2010	Woking	Keiran Hamill	78

Autumn Scratch Medal
American Bar Association Cup

From 1958 the winner of the scratch medal at the Autumn Meeting has won the American Bar Association Cup which was presented by the American Bar Association at its match with the Society at the Berkshire in 1957.

1949	P. Marriage	Wentworth	80
1950	F.R. Furber	Worplesdon	78
1951	P. Marriage	Sundridge Park	76
1952	R.H.R.McGill	Woking	78
1953	No record		
1954	J.D. Kerr	Beaconsfield	78
1955	F.R. Furber	Swinley Forest	74
1956–57	No record		
1958	H.W. Meaby	Royal Wimbledon	74
1959	K. Havard	Berkshire	72
1960	G. Cottam	Sunningdale	79
1961	F.R. Furber	Royal Ashdown Forest	76
1962	P.M. Armitage	West Hill	73
1963	P. Marriage	New Zealand	78
1964	G. Watson and M.A. Blok	West Sussex	79
1965	M.A. Blok	Burhill	75
1966	M.A. Blok	Coombe Hill	77
1967	M.A. Blok	Addington	74
1968	J.J.N. Caplan*	Royal Ashdown Forest	
1969	J.J.N. Caplan*	West Sussex	
1970	J.J.N. Caplan*	Woking	
1971	J.J.N. Caplan*	Sunningdale	
1972	J.J.N. Caplan*	Burhill	
1973	J.J.N. Caplan*	Moor Park	
1974	J.T.L. Watson	Walton Heath	76
1975	J.T.L. Watson	Wentworth	81
1976	J.T.L. Watson	Royal Wimbledon	74
1977	J.J.N. Caplan	Sunningdale	75
1978	B.G.Streather	Berkshire	72
1979	K.S. Gallon	New Zealand	76
1980	J.J.N. Caplan	Walton Heath	75
1981	J.J.N. Caplan	Berkshire	76
1982	B.G. Streather	Worplesdon	75
1983	J.J.N. Caplan	New Zealand	69
1984	J.J.N. Caplan	Berkshire	77
1985	B.G. Streather	Walton Heath	78
1986	B.G. Streather	Worplesdon	74
1987	K.S. Gallon	Berkshire	78
1988	B.G. Streather	Worplesdon	77
1989	D.G. Choyce	Royal Ashdown Forest	75
1990	Roger Davies	Royal Wimbledon	78
1991	John Elgee	Walton Heath	73
1992	Jeremy Caplan	Worplesdon	72
1993	Justyn Jagger	Royal Ashdown Forest	77
1994	Mark Clark	Royal Wimbledon	80
1995	Lance Conway	Walton Heath	82
1996	Julian Walton	Worplesdon	77
1997	Anthony Surtees	Royal Ashdown Forest	86

1998	Jeremy Caplan	Royal Wimbledon	74
1999	Andrew Brown	Walton Heath	86
2000	Jeremy Caplan	Worplesdon	77
2001	Anthony Surtees	Royal Ashdown Forest	
2002	Jeremy Caplan	Royal Wimbledon	75
2003	Harry Anderson	Walton Heath	81
2004	Keith Gallon	Worplesdon	77
2005	Roger Davies	Royal Ashdown Forest	81
2006	Steven Turnbull	Royal Wimbledon	80
2007	Tim Spillane	New Zealand	80
2008	Roger Davies	Worplesdon	79
2009	Philip Langford	Royal Wimbledon	77

Jeremy Caplan* recalled winning at least four (and possibly all six) of the Autumn scratch medals between 1968 to 1973. For the purposes of this record his name is shown in each year. What is certain is that the winner in these years failed to get the Cup engraved with his name and score.

Stoneham Porringer

The Stoneham Porringer is an inter-firm foursomes handicap event. The Porringer was presented by Robert Stoneham to the City of London Solicitors' Company in 1938, and is played for at the Autumn Meeting.

1947	Markby, Stewart & Wadesons (F.G. Petch and L.C. Bullock)
1948	Markby, Stewart & Wadesons (F.G. Petch and L.C. Bullock)
1949	Markby, Stewart & Wadesons (F.G. Petch and L.C. Bullock)
1950	Slaughter and May (F.R. Furber and P. Marriage)
1951	Clifford-Turner & Co (R. Clifford-Turner and F.L. Perkins)
1952	E.F. Turner & Sons (W.R. Carr and R.H.R. McGill)
1953	Slaughter and May (P. Marriage and T.P. Walmsley)
1954	E.F. Turner & Sons (W.R. Carr and R.H.R. McGill)
1955	Lovell, White & King (B.L.B. Hutchings and G.J.B. Hutchings)
1956	Lovell, White & King (F. Williamson and A.R. Nieland)
1957	Clifford-Turner & Co (R. Clifford-Turner and F.L. Perkins)
1958	Lovell, White & King (B.L.B. Hutchings and A.R. Nieland)

1959	Nabarro, Nathanson & Co (L.M. Nathanson and F.J.N. Nabarro)
1960	Slaughter and May (P. Marriage and T.P. Walmsley)
1961	Lovell, White & King (F. Williamson and A.R. Nieland)
1962	Norton, Rose, Botterell & Roche (P.M. Armitage and A.C. Surtees)
1963	Slaughter and May (G.B. Inglis and D.C. Macdonald)
1964	Nabarro, Nathanson & Co (L.M. Nathanson and F.J.N. Nabarro
1965	Clifford-Turner & Co (J.G. Hopton and F.R. Furber)
1966	Arthur Blok & Channon (A.J.R. Blok and M.A. Blok)
1967	Nabarro, Nathanson & Co (L.M. Nathanson and F.J.N. Nabarro)
1968	Herbert Smith & Co (J.F. Goble and M. Ellis)
1969	Lovell, White & King (H.S. Storrs and T.P.D. Ward)
1970	Masons (J.D. Watney and J.A. Watney)
1971	Masons (J.D. Watney and J.A. Watney)
1972	Masons (J.D. Watney and J.A. Watney)
1973	Slaughter and May (T.A. Kinnersley and L.C.J. Wilcox)
1974	Masons (J.D. Watney and J.A. Watney)

1975	Lovell, White & King (G.K. Toland and M.D. Stanford-Tuck)		2000	Linklaters & Paines (R.F. Wheen and C. Johnson-Gilbert)
1976	Allen & Overy (R.G. Davies and J.S. Rink)		2001	CMS Cameron McKenna (P.M. Hewes and A. Jones)
1977	Allen & Overy (K.M.T. Ryan and G.D. Hudson)		2002	CMS Cameron McKenna (P.M. Hewes and A. Jones)
1978	Stephenson Harwood (J.W. Jeffrey and J.M. Jefferson)		2003	Richards Butler (F.J. Donagh and T.E. Watts)
1979	Linklaters & Paines (S.M.Turnbull and J.G.H. Campbell)		2004	Linklaters (S.M. Turnbull and R.F. Wheen)
1980	Slaughter and May (M. Read and H.C. Rumbelow)		2005	Farrer & Co (W.J. Furber and J. Carleton)
1981	Andrade & Mills (R. D. Andrade and D.S. Mills)		2006	Weil, Gotshal & Manges (J. Cousins and D. McCahill)
1982	Norton Rose Botterell & Roche (A.C. Surtees and J.N.L. Chalton)		2007	Gordon Dadds & Co (H.J.W. Elder and D.W.H. Ruck)
1983	Norton Rose Botterell & Roche (A.C. Surtees and J.N.L. Chalton)		2008	Goodman Derrick (P.J.D. Langford and D. Edwards)
1984	Lane & Partners (K.S. Gallon and R.W. Venables)		2009	Gordons (P.D. Hole and D. Cull)
1985	Masons (J.A. Watney and B.O. Lloyd)			

1986 Masons
(J.A. Watney and B.O. Lloyd)

1987 Norton Rose Botterell & Roche
(A.C. Surtees and J.N.L. Chalton)

1988 Edward Lewis & Co
(P.J.D. Langford and J. Rutter)

1989 Church Adams Tatham
(T.G. Arnold and J.J. Elgee)

1990 Norton Rose
(J.N.L. Chalton & A.C. Surtees)

1991 Masons
(J.A. Watney & B.O. Lloyd)

1992 Masons
(J.A. Watney & B.O. Lloyd)

1993 Norton Rose
(J.N.L. Chalton and
P.L. Williams)

1994 Cameron Markby Hewitt
(P.M. Hewes and A. Jones)

1995 Cameron Markby Hewitt
(P.M. Hewes and A. Jones)

1996 Cameron Markby Hewitt
(P.M. Hewes and A. Jones)

1997 Cameron Markby Hewitt
(P.M. Hewes and A. Jones)

1998 Linklaters & Paines
(R.F. Wheen and
C. Johnson-Gilbert)

1999 Farrer & Co
(W.J. Furber and J.A. Gordon)

Riddell Challenge Cup

The Riddell Challenge Cup is the Society's oldest trophy. It was presented by George Riddell in 1905 and was originally played as a handicap matchplay event (sometimes with a 36 hole final) after initial qualification at the Summer Meeting. It is now awarded as a handicap prize at the Spring Meeting for Society members aged 50 or over.

1905	J. Hall
1906	H. Mossop
1907	H. Mossop
1908	H.W. Patey
1909	F. Carver
1910	J. Hall
1911	A.J. Lamb
1912	E. Glenshaw
1913	H.B.W. Foulger
1914	J. Woodhouse
1915–18	War
1919	T. Rothwell Haslam
1920	B. Trayton Kenward
1921	E.S. Trehearne
1922	B. Trayton Kenward
1923	Arnold Carter
1924	B. Trayton Kenward
1925	C.H. Hornby
1926	Sydney Newman
1927	D. Williams

1928	F. Fernihough		1992	Bill Farrer
1929	R.W. Ripley		1993	Arfon Jones
1930	C.F. Rowlands		1994	Jeremy Caplan
1931	C.R. Steele		1995	Clive Rumbelow
1932	K.M. Beaumont		1996	Adrian Watney
1933	E.H. Coe		1997	Martyn Gowar
1934	R.C. Bolton		1998	Peter Morley-Jacob
1935	E.H. Coe		1999	David Wyld
1936	B.M. Patey		2000	Anthony Surtees
1937	Sam Cook		2001	Hugh Elder
1938	J.L. De La Cour		2002	David Wright
1939–48	No Competition		2003	Andrew Daws
1949	D.I.C. Cooke		2004	Harry Anderson
1950	T.F.P. Martin		2005	Christopher Johnson-Gilbert
1951	L.G.D. Loft		2006	Brian Meaby
1952	H.W. Meaby		2007	Ian Elder
1953	No record		2008	Peter Hewes
1954	J.D. Haslam		2009	Brian Meaby
1955	F.G. Petch		2010	Richard Grandison
1956	R. Woolf			
1957	H.F. Bathurst Brown			
1958	L.G.D. Loft and R. Woolf			

Sir Joseph Hood Challenge Cup

The Sir Joseph Hood Challenge Cup was presented by Sir Joseph Hood, President of the Society 1922–1924, and was originally the prize for the Society's Spring singles matchplay knockout (the earliest event). After the Second World War it became a prize at the Society's meeting and is now awarded for the best handicap score at the Spring Meeting.

1959	H.W. Meaby			
1960	E.A.S. Brooks			
1961	P.M. Armitage			
1962	D.O. Smith			
1963	G.P.O'N. Pearson		1919	A.M. Longhurst
1964	D.O. Smith		1920	J. Woodhouse
1965	D.H. Haslam		1921	Sydney Newman
1966	J.R.E. Drooglever		1922	J.F. Ratford
1967	J. Chambres		1923	Arnold Carter
1968	J.D. Watney		1924	F. Burgis
1969	G.P.O'N. Pearson		1925	E. Cripwell
1970	H.C.E. Johnson		1926	F.G. Petch
1971	Hidden by Henry Johnson		1927	S. Cook
1972			1928	R.W. Ripley
1973			1929	H.P.T. Lattey
1974	T.F.P. Martin		1930	E.A.S. Brooks
1975/6	Not Awarded		1931	R.W. Ripley
1977	J.R.N. Holdsworth		1932	R. Woolf
1978	T.F.P. Martin		1933	S. Cook
1979	J. Geils		1934	J.L. de la Cour
1980	H.S. Maxwell-Wood		1935	C.H. Hornby
1981	F.M. Emmett		1936	W.L. Pengelly
1982	F.A. Barnsdale		1937–47	No Competition
1983	P.M. Davies		1948	W.L. Pengelly
1984	J. Geils		1949	W.L. Pengelly
1985	P.J. Morley-Jacob		1950	G.S. Wheatcroft
1986	R.F. Gardner			
1987	E.A.S. Brooks			
1988	C. Clogg			
1989	F.A. Barnsdale			
1990	Anthony Surtees			
1991	Andrew Gerry			

1951	E.F.J. Perkins		2004	Andrew Daws
1952	H.C.E. Johnson		2005	Peter Hewes
1953	G. Vaughan		2006	William King
1954	H.W. Meaby		2007	Tim Watts
1955	J.M. Beharrell		2008	Adam Walker
1956	D.I.C. Cooke)		2009	Ben Thorne
	T.F.P. Martin) (tie)		2010	Adam Walker
1957	J.E.C. Perry			

Ellis Cunliffe Challenge Vase

The Ellis Cunliffe Challenge Vase was pre-sented by Sir Ellis Cunliffe, President of the Society 1914–1921. It was originally played as a singles handicap matchplay knockout. Since 1949 it has been awarded as a foursomes handicap prize and is now played for at the Autumn Meeting.

1958	J.L. Payne			
1959	D. Brooke-Hitching			
1960	D.H. Haslam		1919	H. Francis
1961	M.A. Blok		1920	S. Newman
1962	J.M. Beharrell		1921	J.A. Attenborough
1963	E.A.S. Brooks		1922	H. Forbes White
1964	J.L. Ward		1923	R.W. Ripley
1965	E.A.S. Brooks		1924	J. Hall
1966	A.D. Perriman		1925	L.W. Webster
1967	F.J.N. Nabarro		1926	R.E. Johnson
1968	R. Hayes		1927	R.W. Ripley
1969	B.L.B. Hutchings		1928	W.D. Robinson
1970	G.K. Toland		1929	T.E. St. C. Daniell
1971	J.A. Watney		1930	C.F. Rowlands
1972	M.T. Welchman		1931	S. Cook
1973	E.A.S. Brooks		1932	J.L. de la Cour
1974	J.J.N. Caplan		1933	F. G. Petch
1975	J.D. Watney		1934	R. E. Allen
1976	J.D. Watney		1935	P.D. Franks
1977	J.D. Watney		1936	S. Jennings
1978	J.R. Valdinger		1937	D. J. McArthur
1979	J.M. Bishop		1938–48	No Competition
1980	J.R.N. Holdsworth		1949	E.A.S. Brooks and R.P. Gladstone
1981	A.C. Surtees		1950	No record
1982	P.M. Davies		1951	J.E.B. Rae and H. Mott
1983	J.N.L. Chalton		1952	D.I.C. Cooke and T.F.P. Martin
1984	J.G. Williams		1953	No record
1985	D.G. Choyce		1954	H.W. Meaby and R. Woolf
1986	P.J. Morley-Jacob		1955	J.D. Kerr and P.M. Armitage
1987	C. Millerchip		1956	No record
1988	Nigel Bennett		1957	No record
1989	Neil Hyman		1958	B.J.B. Hutchings and
1990	Nick Downie			A.R.Nieland
1991	Michael Mitchell		1959	No record
1992	Michael Mitchell		1960	P. Marriage and T.P. Walmsley
1993	Howard Gill		1961	F. Williamson and A.R. Nieland
1994	Nigel Bennett		1962	J.G. Parker and C.M. Clough
1995	Christopher Johnson-Gilbert		1963	P.M. Armitage and S. Soames
1996	Nigel Bennett			
1997	Barrie Lloyd			
1998	Ian Goldie			
1999	Jo Rickard			
2000	Frank Donagh			
2001	Christopher Johnson-Gilbert			
2002	Jack Riddy			
2003	Ellie Evans			

1964	M. Ellis and A.R. Nieland	2007	Richard Venables and Holly Venables
1965	F.R. Furber and J.G. Hopton	2008	Philip Langford and David Edwards
1966	J. Chambres and A.D. Perriman	2009	Patrick Hole and David Cull
1967	F.J.N. Nabarro and L.M. Nathanson		
1968	J.F. Goble and M. Ellis		
1969	H.S. Storrs and T.P.D. Ward		
1970	J.D. Watney and J.A. Watney		

Evelyn Jones Foursome Challenge Cups

The Evelyn Jones Foursome Challenge Cups were presented by F Evelyn Jones in 1926 and are now awarded for the best handicap foursomes score at the Spring Meeting.

1971	J.D. Watney and J.A. Watney		
1972	J.D. Watney and J.A. Watney		
1973	L.C.J. Wilcox and T.A. Kinnersley		
1974	R.F. Gardner and J.J.N. Caplan		
1975	R.F. Gardner and J.J.N. Caplan		
1976	R.G. Davies and J.S. Rink	1927	S. Newman and F. Burgis
1977	G.D. Hudson and K.M.T. Ryan	1928	B. Trayton Kenward and H. Robson Sadler
1978	J.W. Jeffrey and J.M. Jefferson	1929	R.E. Johnson and C. Bowen
1979	B.O. Lloyd and R.A. Griffiths	1930	H. Forbes White and C.F. Rowlands
1980	N.M. Curtis and M. Loup	1931	B. Trayton Kenward and A.H. Leathart
1981	J.J.N. Caplan and P.M. Davies	1932	W.T. Watkins Birts and G.E.H. Reader
1982	A.G. Benzie and P.J.D. Langford	1933	J.A. Attenborough and Arnold Carter
1983	J.J.N. Caplan and R.F. Gardner	1934	R.F. Ripley and R.W. Ripley
1984	K.S. Gallon and R.W. Venables	1935	E.H. Coe and S. Newman
1985	J.A. Watney and B.O. Lloyd	1936	N.F. Boyes and C.S. Slingsby
1986	J.A. Watney and B.O. Lloyd	1937	Malcolm Clark and S.K. Nichols
1987	R. Peryer and P. Ralfs	1938	F.G. Petch and E.A.S. Brooks
1988	P.J.D. Langford and J.J. Rutter	1939	F.G. Petch and E.A.S. Brooks
1989	T.G. Arnold and J.J. Elgee	1940–47	No Competition
1990	A.J. Dixon and A.J. McCrae	1948	E.P. Shaw and B.L.B. Hutchings
1991	Adrian Watney and Barrie Lloyd	1949	E. Hyams and F.R. Hamp
1992	Tim Arnold and Hugh Elder	1950	N.M. Baldwin and C.J.G. Woolley
1993	Jonathan Chalton and Paul Williams	1951	D.I.C. Cooke and T.F.P. Martin
1994	Peter Hewes and Arfon Jones	1952	D. Brooke-Hutchings and P.F.C. Lomax
1995	Martin Read and Clive Rumbelow	1953	B.L.B. Hutchings and J.E.B. Rae
1996	Peter Hewes and Arfon Jones	1954	T.G. Bennett and J.D. Kerr
1997	Christopher Millerchip and Adam Walker	1955	H.W. Meaby and R. Woolf
1998	Justin Walkey and Brinsley Nicholson	1956	H.W. Meaby and R. Woolf
1999	Brinsley Nicholson and Alan Black	1957	H.W. Meaby and R. Woolf
2000	Richard Wheen and Christopher Johnson-Gilbert	1958	L.M. Nathanson and F.J.N. Nabarro
2001	Christopher Johnson-Gilbert and Andrew Daws	1959	T.G. Bennett and M.F. West
2002	Arfon Jones and Peter Hewes	1960	P. Marriage and T.P. Walmsley
2003	Andrew Dixon and Chris Millerchip	1961	G. Vaughan and N.W. Roberts
2004	Mike Boswell and Arfon Jones	1962	A.R. Nieland and E.J.B. Hutchings
2005	Steven Turnbull and Keith Gallon	1963	J.K.H. Havard and G.R.E. Wallis
2006	Tom Hawes and Keith Gallon	1964	A.R. Nieland and G. Cottam

1965	J.R.E. Drooglever and W.R. Taylor	2006	Roger Davies and Christopher Johnson-Gilbert
1966	L.M. Nathanson and F.J.N. Nabarro	2007	Tim Watts and Frank Donagh
1967	J.J.N. Caplan and R. Hayes	2008	Jeremy Caplan and John Rink
1968	P.M. Armitage and A.C. Surtees	2009	William King and Stuart Murray
1969	P.L. Gardner and R.F. Gardner	2010	Toby Hornett and Nick Edbrooke
1970	No record		
1971	No record		
1972	No record		

1973 J.R. Weller and M. Hutchings
1974 R.F. Gardner and R.G. Hayes
1975 R.F. Gardner and J.J.N. Caplan
1976 R.H. Burleigh and J.J.N. Caplan
1977 T.M. Hawes and J.R.N. Holdsworth
1978 K.S. Gallon and C.R.L. James
1979 B.G. Streather and C. Travers
1980 R.F. Wheen and P.S. Farren
1981 J.J.N. Caplan and P.M. Davies
1982 C.S. Ranson and B.G. Streather
1983 A.G. Benzie and P.J.D. Langford
1984 A.C. Surtees and J.N.L. Chalton
1985 S.C. Jones and D.G. Choyce
1986 E.A.S. Brooks and I.T.G. Lambert
1987 M. Read and H.C. Rumbelow
1988 B.G. Streather and C.S. Ranson
1989 J.N.L. Chalton and P.L. Williams
1990 Anthony Penna and Derek Randall
1991 Nick Downie and David Wyld
1992 John Clark and Charles Ranson
1993 Philip Langford and Jeremy Rutter
1994 Michael Boswell and Hugh Elder
1995 Alistair Macrae and Nigel Bennett
1996 Keith Gallon and Bill Farrer
1997 Christopher Millerchip and Adam Walker
1998 Richard Grandison and Bill Richards
1999 Julian Walton and John Hargrove
2000 Richard Grandison and Bill Richards
2001 Christopher Johnson-Gilbert and Keith Gallon
2002 David Hunt and James Furber
2003 Richard Grandison and Bill Richards
2004 Martyn Gowar and Jack Riddy
2005 Peter Morley-Jacob and James Gordon

Richardson Sadler Challenge Cup

The Richardson Sadler Challenge Cup was presented in 1929 by H. Robson Sadler to be competed for by members with a handicap of 11 or under. It is now awarded for the best handicap score at the Autumn meeting with no handicap limit.

1929 G.A. Collins
1930 W.R. Taylor
1931–32 J.L. de la Cour
1933 F.G. Petch
1934 R.E. Allen
1935 W.B. Enever
1936 W.B. Enever
1937 N.F. Boyes
1938–48 No Competition
1949 E.A.S. Brooks
1950 No record
1951 T.F.P. Martin
1952 R. Woolf
1953 No record
1954 E.A.S. Brooks
1955 G.J.B. Hutchings
1956 No record
1957 No record
1958 R. Chamberlain
1959 No record
1960 D.H. Haslam
1961 H.F. Bathurst Brown
1962 F.A. Barnsdale
1963 E.A.S. Brooks
1964 E.A.S. Brooks
1965 F.R. Furber
1966 J. Chambres
1967 J.A.P. Wilson
1968 J.D. Watney
1969 E.A.S. Brooks
1970 No record
1971 No record
1972 No record
1973 T.A. Kinnersley
1974 A.J.R. MacKay
1975 D. Mills

1976	R.W. Venables	1983	F.A. Barnsdale
1977	J.M. Bishop	1984	E.A.S. Brooks
1978	H.C.E. Johnson	1985	R.F. Gardner/R.E. Allen (tied)
1979	M.R. Seabrook	1986	F.A. Barnsdale
1980	J.N.L. Chalton	1987	R.F. Gardner
1981	I.W. Goldie	1988	E.A.S. Brooks
1982	H.C. Rumbelow	1989	W.O. Farrer
1983	A.C. Surtees	1990	Peter Morley-Jacob
1984	R.W. Venables	1991	Anthony Surtees
1985	A.C. Surtees	1992	Peter Marriage
1986	H.J.W. Elder	1993	Clive Rumbelow
1987	A.C. Surtees	1994	Henry Johnson
1988	P.J.D. Langford	1995	Peter Morley-Jacob
1989	J.A. Watney	1996	Barrie Lloyd
1990	Charles Crick	1997	Andrew Gerry
1991	Andrew Dixon	1998	Martin Read
1992	Barney Hearden	1999	Barrie Lloyd
1993	Michael Mitchell	2000	Jonathan Chalton
1994	Hugh Elder	2001	Andrew Daws
1995	Arfon Jones	2002	Anthony Surtees
1996	A.M.Elliott	2003	Frank Donagh
1997	Arfon Jones	2004	Frank Donagh
1998	Christopher Johnson-Gilbert	2005	Arfon Jones
1999	James Furber	2006	Richard Harvey
2000	Michael Mitchell	2007	Anthony Surtees
2001	Christopher Johnson-Gilbert	2008	Anthony Surtees
2002	Philip Langford	2009	Brian Meaby
2003	Anthony Surtees		
2004	Brian Gegg		
2005	Tim Watts		
2006	Dominic McCahill		
2007	Brian Gegg		
2008	Barrie Lloyd		
2009	Andrew Daws		

Liberty Bowl

The Liberty Bowl was presented by Leslie Nathanson and is awarded to the winners of an inter-firm foursomes handicap competition at the Spring Meeting. One of the players must be under 45 (under 35 before 2005). Since 2005 the winners are determined by taking the aggregate of their individual morning scores as well as their afternoon foursomes score.

Armada Dish

The Armada Dish was presented by Leslie Nathanson as a President's Trophy and is awarded as a handicap prize at the Autumn Meeting for members over 55. The competitors are entitled to add an extra ½ point to the stableford score for each year over 55.

1974	E.A.S. Brooks
1975	E.A.S. Brooks
1976	F.A. Barnsdale
1977	L.M. Nathanson
1978	E.A.S. Brooks
1979	E.A.S. Brooks
1980	J.A.P. Wilson
1981	T.F.P. Martin
1982	E.A.S. Brooks

1987	Norton Rose Botterell & Roche Jonathan Chalton and Paul Williams
1988	Streather & Co Bruce Streather and Charles Ranson
1989	Norton Rose Jonathan Chalton and Paul Williams
1990	Simmons & Simmons David Pryor and Mark Clark
1991	Allen & Overy Roger Davies and Richard Gray
1992	Linklaters & Paines

	Steven Turnbull and
	Richard Good
1993	Allen & Overy
	John Rink and Richard Hough
1994	Herbert Smith
	Justyn Jagger and Tom Cowgill
1995	Cameron Markby Hewitt
	Arfon Jones and James Tully
1996	Nabarro Nathanson
	David Wright and
	John Cumpson
1997	Farrer & Co
	James Carleton and
	James Furber
1998	Linklaters & Paines
	Christopher Johnson-Gilbert
	and David Barr
1999	Allen & Overy
	Ashley Aylmer and Roger Davies
2000	Allen & Overy
	Ashley Aylmer and Roger Davies
2001	Farrer & Co
	James Furber and David Hunt
2002	Farrer & Co
	James Furber and David Hunt
2003	Lawrence Graham
	Jack Riddy and Martyn Gowar
2004	Lawrence Graham
	Jack Riddy and Martyn Gowar
2005	Farrer & Co
	James Furber and
	Jeremy Gordon
2006	Lawrence Graham
	Jack Riddy and Martyn Gowar
2007	Farrer & Co
	James Furber and
	Jeremy Gordon
2008	Simmons & Simmons
	Andrew Brydon and
	Gregory Brandman
2009	Kennedys
	Matt Andrews and
	David MacLoughlin
2010	Kennedys
	Matt Andrews and
	David MacLoughlin

The Captain's Prize
The Gardner Salver

The Gardner Salver was given to Ray Gardner by his partners to commemorate 50 years with Gordon Dadds & Co., from 1932–1982. Since 1996 the Gardner Salver has been awarded as the Captain's Prize for the best combined stableford handicap score in the Captain's year of office, at the Autumn and Spring meetings.

1996	C N Robertson
1997	Barrie Lloyd
1998	Anthony Surtees
1999	Christopher Johnson-Gilbert
2000	Barrie Lloyd
2001	Christopher Johnson-Gilbert
2002	Christopher Johnson-Gilbert
2003	Philip Langford
2004	Anthony Surtees
2005	Barrie Lloyd
2006	William King
2007	Tim Watts
2008	Christopher Johnson-Gilbert
2009	Stephen Barnard
2010	David Edwards

The Writers' Quaich

The Writers' Quaich was presented by the Writers to the Signet GC in 2004 on the centenary of the Society and is awarded for the best handicap score by a player under 45

2005	Jack Riddy
2006	David Edwards
2007	Jeremy Gordon
2008	Andrew Brydon
2009	Adam Walker
2010	Simon McKnight

City of London Solicitors' Company Challenge Cup

The City of London Solicitors' Company Annual Golf Challenge Cup was presented in 1911 by the Master, Wardens and Court of the Company. It is awarded for the best handicap score at the Spring Meeting by a member of the City of London Solicitors' Company who is also a member of the Society. Before 1931 it was competed for at a separate meeting of the golfers of the Solicitors' Company; in 1931 it was played as a foursomes competition.

1911	C.H. Drayton
1912	J. Barling Purchase
1913	N.H. Aste

Year	Winner	Year	Winner
1925	H.W. Morris	1985	A.C. Surtees
1926	H.W. Morris	1986	R.G. Davies
1927	F.T. Mawby	1987	M. Read
1928	W. Ward Higgs	1988	H.C. Rumbelow
1931	W.T. Watkins Birts and	1989	B.R.N. Nicholson
	F.T. Mawby	1990	Mark Clark
1932	F. le S. Stone	1991	Richard Grandison
1933	F. le S. Stone	1992	Peter Morley-Jacob
1934	W.T. Watkins Birts	1993	Peter Borrowdale
1935	R.C. Bolton	1994	Arfon Jones
1936	R.C. Bolton	1995	Rob McKellar
1937	F.G. Petch	1996	Ian Goldie
1938	W.T. Watkins Birts	1997	Ian Goldie
1939	R.C. Bolton	1998	Christopher Johnson-Gilbert
1940–46	No Competition	1999	Christopher Johnson-Gilbert
1947	F.G. Petch	2000	John Rink
1948	F.G. Petch	2001	Martyn Gowar
1949	F.G. Petch and T.G. Bennett	2002	Steven Turnbull
1950	L.A.D. Martin	2003	John Pike
1951	L.G.D. Croft)	2004	John Pike
	L.A.D. Martin)	2005	Barrie Lloyd
1952	L.G.D. Croft	2006	Michael Boswell
1953	F.G. Petch	2007	Stephen Barnard
1954	L.G.D. Croft	2008	Richard Grandison
1955	F.G. Petch	2009	Arfon Jones
1956	T.G. Bennett	2010	David Edwards
1957	L.G.D. Croft		
1958	L.G.D. Croft		
1959	R. Chamberlain		
1960	T.G. Bennett		
1961	R. Chamberlain		
1962	P.M. Armitage		
1963	L.A.D. Martin		
1964	T.G. Bennett		
1965	W.R. Carr		
1966	A.C. Surtees		
1967	P.M. Armitage		
1968	A.C. Surtees		
1969	No record		
1970	No record		
1971	No record		
1972	P.J. Morley-Jacob		
1973	J.F. Goble		
1974	H.S.Maxwell-Wood		
1975	No record		
1976	C.R.L. James		
1977	H.C. Rumbelow		
1978	A.C. Surtees		
1979	I.W. Goldie		
1980	J.N.L. Chalton		
1981	J.N.L. Chalton		
1982	B.W.D. Richards		
1983	F.J. Donagh		
1984	D.J. Wright		

Match Play Trophy

The Match-Play Trophy was started in 2004, the centenary of the Society. It is a handicap knock-out event. The trophy is a Victorian salver presented by Philip Langford, the organiser.

2004	Jamie Hudson beat Andrew Barrow in the final
2005	Jeremy Caplan beat Stuart Murray
2006	Brian Gegg beat Stuart Murray
2007	Christopher Johnson-Gilbert beat Bill Richards
2008	Tim Russell beat John Hagan
2009	Grant Needham beat Roger Davies

The Claret Jug

The Claret Jug was purchased by the Society as a prize for its matches against representatives of the American Bar Association. In the event, it was only played for once, at Sunningdale in July 1971, when LSGS won 8–4. In 1980 the Claret Jug was presented, in memory of Tommy Walmsley, as the trophy for the match against the Bar and Bench and is kept at Woking GC where the match is played.

Sir Hugh Watson Trophy

The Sir Hugh Watson Trophy was presented by Leslie Nathanson as the prize for the annual match between the Society and the Writers to the Signet GC. The first match was played at Royal St George's in 1961 and the second at Muirfield and this alternation has continued, although the 2009 match was played at Royal Cinque Ports.

1961	LSGS 12 – 6
1962	WSGC 10 ½ – 9 ½
1963	LSGS 17 ½ – 2 ½
1964	LSGS 10 ½ – 7 ½
1965	LSGS 10 ½ – 7 ½
1966	WSGC 7 ½ – 6 ½
1967	Match halved
1968	WSGC 11 – 7
1969	WSGC 10 ½ – 6 ½
1970	WSGC 10 – 8
1971	LSGS 12 ½ – 5 ½
1972	LSGS 10 – 6
1973	LSGS 10 ½ – 9 ½
1974	LSGS 15 – 7
1975	LSGS 10 ½ – 8 ½
1976	WSGC 10 ½ – 9 ½
1977	WSGC 11 ½ – 8 ½
1978	LSGS 11 – 9
1979	LSGS 11 – 9
1980	WSGC 13 ½ – 6 ½
1981	WSGC 11 ½ – 8 ½
1982	WSGC 13 – 7
1983	LSGS 12 ½ – 7 ½
1984	WSGC 4 – 2
	Afternoon matches abandoned
1985	WSGC 11 ½ – 8 ½
1986	WSGC 10 ½ – 9 ½
1987	LSGS 11 ½ – 8 ½
1988	LSGS 11 – 9
1989	LSGS 11 ½ – 7 ½
1990	WSGC 10 ½ – 9 ½
1991	LSGS 13 – 7
1992	WSGC 15 – 5
1993	WSGC 12 ½ – 7 ½
1994	WSGC 10 ½ – 9 ½
1995	LSGS 13 ½ – 6 ½
1996	LSGS 13 ½ – 6 ½
1997	WSGC 10 ½ – 9 ½
1998	WSGC 13 – 7
1999	LSGS 13 – 7
2000	LSGS 11 ½ – 8 ½
2001	LSGS 17 – 3
2002	LSGS 13 – 7
2003	LSGS 13 – 7
2004	LSGS 11 ½ – 8 ½
2005	LSGS 12 ½ – 7 ½
2006	LSGS 11 ½ – 8 ½
2007	LSGS 14 – 6
2008	WSGC 12 ½ – 7 ½
2009	LSGS 11 ½ – 8 ½

East Anglian solicitors

The Society's annual match against the East Anglian solicitors has been played at Aldeburgh since informal beginnings in the mid 1970s.

1977	East Anglia won 5 – 3
1978	East Anglia 7 – 1
1979	LSGS 4 ½ – 3 ½
1980	No record
1981	East Anglia 5 ½ – 4 ½
1982	LSGS 6 – 4
1983	No record
1984	East Anglia 6 ½ – 4 ½
1985	LSGS 7 ½ – 4 ½
1986	LSGS 8 – 4
1987	Match halved 6 – 6
1988	East Anglia 5 ½ – 4 ½
1989	East Anglia 6 ½ – 5 ½
1990	LSGS 6 – 4
1991	LSGS 7 ½ – 4 ½
1992	East Anglia
1993	Match halved
1994	LSGS
1995	East Anglia 9 – 3
1996	Match halved 6 – 6
1997	East Anglia 8 ½ – 3 ½
1998	East Anglia 7 – 4
1999	East Anglia 7 – 5
2000	East Anglia 8 ½ – 3 ½
2001	LSGS 6 ½ – 5 ½
2002	LSGS 9 – 3
2003	East Anglia 6 ½ – 5 ½
2004	Match halved 6 – 6
2005	East Anglia 6 – 5
2006	LSGS 6 ½ – 5 ½
2007	LSGS 6 ½ – 5 ½
2008	East Anglia 7 ½ – 4 ½
2009	LSGS 6 ½ – 4 ½
2010	East Anglia 4 ½ – 3 ½

Index

The index includes names in the main text and captions but not in the Appendices